SIX BASQUE POETS

# SIX BASQUE POETS

Translated from the Basque by
Amaia Gabantxo

Edited and introduced by
Mari Jose Olaziregi,
University of the Basque Country

PUBLICATIONS
2007

Published by Arc Publications
Nanholme Mill, Shaw Wood Road
Todmorden, OL14 6DA, UK
www.arcpublications.co.uk

Design by Tony Ward
Printed by Biddles Ltd
King's Lynn, Norfolk

ISBN-13: 978 1904614 26 5

The publishers are grateful to the authors and
translators and, in the case of previously
published works, to their publishers
for allowing their poems
to be included in this anthology.

Cover design by Pavel Büchler.
The cover illustration by Zumeta © 2007
is reproduced by kind permission of the artist
and with thanks to Jose Luis Agote.

The publishers acknowledge financial assistance
from Arts Council England, Yorkshire

LOTTERY FUNDED

The 'New Voices from Europe and Beyond' anthology series is published in
co-operation with Literature Across Frontiers which receives support
from the Culture 2000 programme of the EU.

LITERATURE
ACROSS
FRONTIERS

Arc Publications 'New Voices from Europe and Beyond'
Series Editor: Alexandra Büchler

The Publishers would particularly like to thank the
Department of Culture, Government of the Basque Country
from whom they have received financial assistance
in the preparation of this volume.

Thanks are also due to the Instituto Cervantes, Manchester
for their help in promoting this volume.

 **Instituto
Cervantes
Manchester**

Poems in this anthology have previously appeared
in the following publications:

### BERNADO ATXAGA

'Trikuarena' (The Tale of the Hedgehog) from *Poemas & Híbridos*
(Madrid: Visor, 1990); 'Adan eta bizitza' (Adam and Life) from Ameztoy,
Vicente et al., *Eliztarrak-mundutarrak: Erremelluriko sainduak
paradisua eta beste lan batzuk: [erakusketa] / Sagrado-profano:
santoral de Remelluri, paraíso y otras obras: [exposición]* / Vicente
Ameztoy; [textuak / textos, Bernardo Atxaga, Fernando Golvano],
(Donostia: K M Arteleku, 2000); 'Elegia' (Elegy) from *Ladinamo* 9 (2004);
'Bizitzak ez du etsitzen' (Life) from *Poemas & Híbridos* (Madrid: Vi-
sor, 1990); 'Bizitza bizitza da' (Life is Life) from Muguruza, Jabier,
*Abenduak 29* (Madrid: Resistencia, 2005); 'Canción tonta' (Silly Song)
from *Poemas & Híbridos* (Madrid: Visor, 1990); 'Egun finlandiar bat'
(A Finnish Day) from *Nueva Etiopía* (Madrid: El Europeo, 1996).

### RIKARDO ARREGI

'Kalean erori paperak' (Papers on the Pavement), 'Lur lokartua III'
(The Sleeping Land III), '66 lerro hiri sitiatuan' (66 Lines from the City
under Siege), 'Edonon ilargia' (The Moon Anywhere), 'Onassis taberna'
(Onassis Tavern), 'Musikaren lurraldeak II' (Territories of Music II) and
'Zin egite telefonikoak' (Telephone Promises) from *Kartografia*
(Donostia: Alberdania-Elkarlanean, 1998); 'Amodiozko poema I' (Love
Poem I) from *Talaia* (1999).

### FELIPE JUARISTI

"Berdin da Mendebaldea eta Ekialdea…" (It makes no difference, mix-
ing West with East…) from *Denbora, nostalgia* (Donostia: Baroja,
1984); 'Smoothy' from *Hiriaren melankolia* (Donostia: Baroja, 1986);
'Metropolis 2' from *Laino artean zelatari* (Irun: Alberdania, 1993);
'Panamako Istmoa' (The Isthmus of Panama), 'Vanitas Vanitatis' (Van-
ity of Vanities) and 'Perspektiva Nevsky' (Nevsky Propsect) from *Laino
artean zelatari* (Irun: Alberdania, 1993); 'Auschwitz', 'Baratzain' (Gar-
dener) and 'Geografia' (Geography) from *Galderen geografia* (Irun:
Alberdania, 1997); "Rembrandtek infinitua nahi du pintatu…" (Rembrandt
wants to paint infinity…) from *Begi ikarak* (Donostia: Erein, 2004).

**MIREN AGUR MEABE**

'Kodea' (Code), 'Memoria ez galtzeko oharrak (2)' (How to avoid Memory Loss (2)), 'Ohar laburrak (1)' (Brief Notes (1)), "Bildu nire igitai-ilargi izoztuaren jario zurbila..." (Scoop the flow of my pale half-moon...), 'Galdeketa' (Questions), "Basalarrosek..." (Wild roses...) and 'Gauza konkretuak' (Concrete Things) from *Azalaren kodea* ( Zarautz: Susa, 2000); 'Inurria (II)' (The Ant (II)) from *Poetikak & Poemak* (Donostia: Erein, 2005).

**JOSEBA SARRIONANDIA**

'Bitakora kaiera' (Nautical Logbook), 'Hil egin da organista' (The Organist is Dead) and 'Etxera itzuli' (Return Home) from *Izuen gordelekuetan barna* (Bilbo: Pott, 1981); 'Tren luze bat' (A Long Train), 'Zapata hautsi pila bat' (A Pile of Broken Shoes), 'Preso egon denaren gogoa' (The Ex-Prisoner's Mind) and 'Literatura eta iraultza' (Literature and Revolution) from *Marinel zaharrak* (Donostia: Elkar, 1987); 'Iheslariaren ekipaia' (A Runaway's Luggage), 'Minotauroarenak' (The Minotaur speaks) and 'Proposamen poetikoa' (Poetic Proposal) from *Hnuy illa nyha majah yahoo (poemak 1985-1995),* (Donostia: Elkar, 1995).

**KIRMEN URIBE**

'Ibaia' (The River), 'Irla' (The Island), 'Bisita' (The Visit) and 'Mahmud' from *Bitartean heldu eskutik* (Zarautz: Susa, 2001); 'Kukua' (The Cuckoo) from *Zaharregia, txikiegia agian* (Donostia: Gaztelupeko hotsak, 2003); 'Txoriak neguan' (Birds in Winter) from *Poetikak & Poemak* (Donostia: Erein, 2005); 'Gauza perfektuak' (Perfect Things) from *Zaharregia, txikiegia agian* (Donostia: Gaztelupeko hotsak, 2003); 'Ezin esan' (The Unsayable), 'Aparte-apartean' (Way Beyond) and 'Maiatza' (May) from *Bitartean heldu eskutik* (Zarautz: Susa, 2001).

Arc Publications would like to thank the publishers of the above poems for granting permission to reproduce them in the present volume.

The following poems are published for the first time
in this anthology:
**BERNARDO ATXAGA:** 'Zebrak eta heriotza' (Death and the Zebras) and 'Egunak ba doatzi' (The Days go by); **RIKARDO ARREGI:** 'Gilen Akitaniakoak bezala' (Like Gilen of Aquitaine); **MIREN AGUR MEABE:** 'Ametsetako urak III' (Water Dreams III) and 'Eolia III' (Aeolia).

Finally, especial thanks are due to Alexandra Büchler, Director of Literature Across Frontiers, for her vision in conceiving the 'New Voices from Europe and Beyond' anthology series.

# CONTENTS

The present anthology is the second in a new and much-needed series which brings contemporary international poetry to English-language readers. It is not by accident that the tired old phrase about poetry being 'lost in translation' came out of an English-speaking environment, out of a tradition that has always felt remarkably uneasy about translation. Yet poetry can be, and *is*, 'found' in translation; in fact, any good translation *reinvents* the poetry of the original. We should never lose sight of the fact that translation is the outcome of a dialogue – between two cultures, two languages and two poetic traditions, between collective as well as individual imaginations – a dialogue conducted by two voices, that of the poet and of the translator, which are joined by a third participant in the process of interpretative reading.

It is this dialogue that is so important to writers in countries and regions where translation has always been an integral part of the literary environment and has played a role in the development of their literary tradition and poetics. Writing without having read poetry from other cultures would be unthinkable for the poets in the anthologies of this new series, many of whom are also accomplished translators, for, as well as considering poetry in translation part of their own literary background, they also regard it as an important source of inspiration.

While this series aims to keep a finger on the pulse of the here-and-now of contemporary poetry by presenting the work of a small number of contemporary poets, each collection, edited by a guest editor, has its own focus and rationale for the selection of the poets and poems to be included. *Six Basque Poets* makes available to the English-language reader the work of leading poets writing in Euskera, including the well-known novelist Bernardo Atxaga as well as outstanding representatives of the younger generation who started publishing at the turn of the millennium. These younger writers have ushered in a new confidence in Basque writing and publishing, a territory still largely unknown to an international readership but one certainly worth exploring; for a journey through this territory not only opens up new and unexpected horizons but also eventually leads to a greater understanding of a culture hitherto obscured from sight by political struggle for recognition and autonomy.

I would like to thank those who made this edition possible; above all, Mari Jose Olaziregi, for her tireless promotion of Basque writing and culture and her informative introduction to this volume, and Amaia Gabantxo for translations which allow the voices of these poets to speak to us with undiminished intellectual and poetic power.

*Alexandra Büchler*

> *Poetry is not an uncommon activity, it is playing at restoring
> the language, looking at new ways of making connections,
> composing imperfect works. It is a human endeavour as
> dignified as making lemonade.*
>
> JOSEBA SARRIONANDIA[1]

## THE TERRITORY OF BASQUE LITERATURE

Claudio Magris has said that all writers are frontier writers, whether they know it or not; that in the end writing, the act of ravelling and unravelling the world to make sense of it, is a continuous reassessment of frontiers. Textual and generic frontiers all writers must navigate, and frontiers which, as in the case of a minority literature such as Basque, signal the difficulty of getting over geographical limitations, of making oneself heard.

Although Basque is the oldest language in Western Europe and is only spoken by approximately 700,000 people, this should not get in the way of our literature being better known around the world; but the fact is that the socio-historical situation of our language has had a great influence on the development of literature written in Basque. It was with this in mind that Harkaitz Cano, a contemporary Basque writer, speaking during the 2000 Frankfurt Book Fair, quoted from Auden's well-known *Letters from Iceland* and compared the isolation of islands to the isolation of Basque literature.

And because I am introducing an anthology of poetry, or a "memorable speech", as Auden would say, I should mention that Auden's centenary – which took place in 2007 – was celebrated in the Basque Country with the publication of a volume of new translations of his poems into Basque. This and many other seminal authors' works have been translated into Basque in the last thirty-odd years. This indicates that the isolation I have mentioned does not apply to the constant dialogue between the particular and the universal that every literary exercise demands. In this respect, the fact that Basque is an isolate language – in other words, unrelated to all other living languages – has not stopped it from incorporating words from diverse lexical origins, and the same has happened to literature in Basque. Bernardo Atxaga, one of the poets included in this anthology, put it as follows in his book *Obabakoak* (1988), the most successful Basque novel to date: "These days nothing can be said to be peculiar to one place or person. The world is everywhere and Euskal Herria is no longer just Euskal Herria but (...) the place where the world takes the name of Euskal Herria".[2] The Basque language, *Euskara*, defines our place in the world, our territory, as George Steiner would

---

[1] Quoted in *Metamorphoses,* Spring / Fall 2004, vol. 12, p. 22.
[2] Atxaga, Bernardo, *Obabakoak* (New York: Vintage, 1994), p. 324.

say. For this reason and despite the many difficulties encountered along the way, Basque people continue to hold tight to that territory.

*Euskara* is one of the three languages we speak within the geographic confines[3] of the Basque Country, and the one that gives it its name and its essence: *Euskal Herria*, the Basque country's name in Basque, means "the land of *Euskara* speakers". It is estimated that, at present, thanks to Basque radio and television (see www.eitb.com), approximately 87 million homes in Europe and three million in the United States have access to *Euskara*. In terms of literary translations, however, the numbers are much more limited. Only 200 titles or so have been translated from Basque into other languages. But the internet has brought new hope and websites have been created for the sole purpose of encouraging the circulation of the existing translations of contemporary Basque literary texts (www.basqueliterature.com and www.basquepoetry.net are two good examples of this).

The first book in history to be published in *Euskara* was a volume of poetry published in 1545. Its title was *Linguae Vasconum Primitiae* and the author's name was Bernard Etxepare. It consisted of fifteen poems dealing with themes such as love and religion and a prose prologue. In it, the author expressed his joy at the possibilities created by the invention of the printing press and his hope that it would help disseminate Basque literature. But it would appear his optimism was excessive, because as it happened, Basque literature took a very different turn from the sixteenth century onwards. The pre-eminence of religious texts was practically absolute. Not until the last decade of the nineteenth century did a new spirit emerge that would transform Basque literature. Poetry was not the only genre, however; novels written in Basque started to appear towards the end of the century. Although religion was not the main subject matter from then on, Basque literature would continue to be a product of extra-literary objectives, such as nationalism, until quite late in the twentieth century. For this reason, for many decades Basque literature existed outside the European Modernist movement – whose aim was to revolutionise language and highlight the fragmented nature of the modern age. In the 1930s, two poets, Xabier Lizardi and Esteban Urkiaga "Lauaxeta", explored the expressive possibilities of Basque through post-symbolist poetics, but it was only in the 1950s that the dialogue with modernity became more firmly established through the

---

[3] The political frontier that divides the Basque country between Spain and France creates different legal situations. After the 1978 Spanish Constitution was approved, Basque was granted the same official status as Spanish. However, this is not the case in the French Basque country, where Basque is not an official language. The consequences of this inequality are clear: the establishment of bilingual education models and the grants available for publishing books in Basque have meant that the Basque literary system is much stronger and more dynamic in the Spanish part of the Basque country.

voices of two poets, Gabriel Aresti (1933-1975) and Jon Mirande (1925-1972).

The Spanish Civil War took place in the intervening years (1936-39); it was a time of severe repression and censorship and many intellectuals were killed or went into exile. After the war, the victorious side established a series of repressive laws. Basque names were forbidden, for example, as were Basque inscriptions on tombstones. During those years Franco exercised tremendous censorship on Basque politics and culture. His measures included forbidding the use of Basque in the street and in schools. It has been said that the post-war generation was the most important generation in the history of Basque literature, because it created something that was much needed at the time – continuity. The most popular genre at the time was poetry, partly because it was easier to publish a couple of poems here or there than to publish a whole book, but also because in the 1940s and '50s it was practically impossible for publishing houses to function normally. This new generation of writers, which emerged in the 1950s, was formed by the above-mentioned poets Gabriel Aresti and Jon Mirande, and the novelist J. L. Alvarez Enparantza who, in 1957, published the first modern Basque novel – the existentialist *Leturiaren egunkari ezkutua* (Leturia's Secret Diary). With this novel Basque literature took a step towards the incorporation of modern European literary ideas, but its main achievement was to free Basque literature from political, religious or folkloric servility – from this point onwards, the aesthetic function would prevail.

Jon Mirande was first to transgress the religious spirit latent in Basque poetry until the 1950s. An exceptional polyglot (he spoke all Celtic languages as well as French, German, English, Dutch, Russian, Hebrew and some others), he started learning Basque at the age of 20. Mitxelena, the renowned Basque philologist, praised the depth of Mirande's cultural knowledge. Echoes of his many and varied philosophical and literary readings (such as the stoics, Nietzsche, Spengler, Poe, Baudelaire, Kafka and Yeats) abound in his prose and poetry. Mirande was a heterodox and a nihilist, and among other things wrote *Haur besotakoa* (The Goddaughter, 1970), a kind of Basque *Lolita*. His poetry was admired for its rhythmic patterns and musicality, its use of alliteration, its daring eroticism and its many cultural references.

Gabriel Aresti was without a doubt one of the most important Basque poets of the second half of the twentieth century. His career as a writer, editor, translator and linguist demonstrated his devotion to Basque culture. He was essential to the next generation: his example and enthusiasm were a great source of inspiration. Authors such as Bernardo Atxaga or Ramon Saizarbitoria have written at length about Aresti's charisma and his importance to Basque letters. He wrote short stories, poetry and drama, and translated authors such as Boccacio, Eliot and Hikmet. The title of his first poetry collection was *Maldan behera* (Downhill, 1960). It was clearly influenced by symbolist poetry and T. S. Eliot. However, it was his move towards socio-political poetry that brought him a wide Basque-speaking readership. The publication of *Harri eta herri* (Stone and Country, 1964) is a landmark in the history of Basque literature, and some of its poems – such as 'Nire aitaren etxea defendituko dut' (I shall defend my father's house) – have been translated into many languages. The poems in *Harri eta herri* take place in an urban environment and are written in free verse; Basque critics at the time praised their modernity, innovative spirit and their left-wing humanism. Harking back to the oral tradition, the poet chose to use simple, direct language to communicate a clear message, and these qualities meant he was widely accepted. For Aresti, poetry was the hammer with which to awaken the sleeping conscience – or, as Gabriel Celaya, a poet friend of his said, a weapon loaded with future. *Harri eta herri* was followed by *Euskal harria* (Basque Stone, 1967) and *Harrizko herri hau* (This Country of Stone, 1971).

In the 1960s, events such as the economic and industrial developments, the establishment of Basque schools (*ikastola*s), the creation of a unified Basque language, political activism against Franco's regime and the campaigns for Basque language learning, created a favourable environment for the development of new literary ideas. It has been said before that the existing cultural orthodoxy of the time was challenged by an emerging cultural and political heterodoxy, heralded by authors such as Aresti, the philologist Koldo Mitxelena (1915-1987) and the sculptor Jorge Oteiza (1908-2003). During these years political and cultural activism went hand in hand. A consequence of this was that socio-political poetry found its best ally in modern Basque song, and especially in the group *Ez dok amairu*, which was formed by poets such as Xabier Lete (b. 1944), Joxean Arze (b. 1939) and Joxe Anjel Irigarai (b. 1942). Around the same time, and linked to this movement of social commitment, a number of female poets emerged, such as Amaia Lasa (b. 1949) and Arantxa Urretabizkaia (b. 1947), who wrote about a poetic reality that had been silenced until then: that of women.

The relevance of poetry to Basque literature became more and more firmly established as time passed, and reached a peak in the 1970s. It is interesting to note that in the years between 1936 and 1975, poetry was the major, canonical genre in Basque literature (it accounted for 27.9% of literary production, as opposed to fiction's 23.8%). But things changed radically after Franco's death in 1975, because from then on, and for the first time in history, the Basque literary system was supported by a legal framework that allowed it to develop unhindered. In the Spanish Basque Country, the adoption of the *Estatuto de Autonomía* (Autonomy Status) in 1979 and the Law for the Normalization of the Use of the Basque Language in 1982 allowed, among other things, the establishment of bilingual educational models and grants for the publication of books in Basque. Thanks to these grants, new publishing houses flourished, and book production increased significantly. In 2005,[4] a total of 1648 books were published; of those, 12.2% were works of literature (247 titles in total). Their distribution according to genre was as follows: 62.3% fiction, 14.5% poetry, 2% drama and 3.2% essays. In recent years, the tendency has been to publish more titles in smaller editions (the average number of books per edition is 1019 in the market for adults).

The present literary system[5] comprises around 300 writers, 17% of which are women. The novel is the star genre, the one that offers the greatest prestige and rewards. Authors such as Ramon Saizarbitoria (b. 1944) and Anjel Lertxundi (b. 1948) experimented with new ideas in this genre – influenced by the Nouveau Roman in the case of Saizarbitoria, and by a continuous search for the renewal of form in the case of Lertxundi.[6] The evolution of the short story from the 1980s onwards also merits a mention. The process of renewal initiated by canonical authors such as Bernardo Atxaga and Joseba Sarrionandia has been continued by contemporary short story writers such as Pello Lizarralde (b. 1956), Iban Zaldua (b. 1966) and Harkaitz Cano (b. 1975).[7]

## MAPPING OUT BASQUE POETRY TODAY: THE PRESENT ANTHOLOGY

Borges wrote[8] that British literature was characteristically insular, in other words, defined by individuals rather than schools. The same could be said about the complex and diverse contemporary Basque poetry scene. Words such as "eclectic" spring to mind when one tries

---

[4] Data provided by the sociologist J. M. Torrealdai in *Jakin*, no. 158, Jan / Feb 2007. Similar data is also available from the president of Euskal Editoreen Elkartea (Association of Basque Publishers), Jorge Giménez, at www.basqueliterature.com/basque/euskalib.

[5] See Olaziregi, M. J., 'The Basque Literary System', in *Waking the Hedgehog. The Literary Universe of Bernardo Atxaga* (Reno: University of Nevada Press, 2005). Translated from Basque by Amaia Gabantxo. This information is also available at: http://www.basqueliterature.com/basque/historia/hogeimende/sarrera.

[6] For more information on Basque narrative see: Olaziregi, M. J., 'The evolution of the Basque Narrative', in M. E. Altisent (co-ord.), *A Companion to the 20th-Century Spanish Novel* (London: Boydell & Brewer Ltd. 'Tamesis Series', 2007). See also: http://www.basqueliterature.com/katalogoak.

[7] See Olaziregi, M. J. (ed.), *An Anthology of Basque Short Stories* (Reno: University of Nevada Press, 2004).

[8] Borges, J. L., *Introducción a la literatura inglesa* (Madrid: Alianza, 1999).

to describe the diversity of voices and poetic schools that populate it. The avant-garde ideas of the 1970s have been left behind, and instead, a variety of tendencies emerge on the horizon of contemporary Basque poetry which include: a wide diversity of poetics (poetics of experience, surrealist poetics, post-symbolist poetics, poetics of silence, etc.); use of various narrative styles; a preference for non-aesthetic poetics that dwell with the quotidian; and an emergence of female voices that reclaim other codes, other universes, based on the female body. In addition, more and more often, audiences enjoy poetic performances that combine poetry with music or other arts. Young contemporary poets especially seem to be influenced by the Beat generation and gritty realism. It is clear that what happened to the other literary genres has also happened to poetry – it has absorbed those characteristics literary critics describe as postmodern: a denial of transcendental meaning; an assertion that all literature is metaliterature in
the end; a non-elitist attitude towards literary creation; use of pastiche; mistrust of language; hybridization of genres; and so on. In other words, Basque poetry displays a tendency towards aesthetic populism and a totally non-auratic attitude to the figure of the poet. There are other contemporary poets worth mentioning apart from those included in this anthology, for instance Koldo Izagirre, Aurelia Arkotxa, Juanjo Olasagarre, Karlos Linazasoro and Harkaitz Cano.

For this anthology I have tried to select poets who, in my opinion, have played a defining role in the development of Basque poetry in the last thirty years, that is, since the arrival (around 1975) of what we have come to refer to as the "democratic age". The poets included in this anthology are Bernardo Atxaga, Joseba Sarrionandia, Felipe Juaristi, Rikardo Arregi, Miren Agur Meabe and Kirmen Uribe. The first three started publishing in the 1970s and 1980s, the last three in the 1990s. All have been endorsed and applauded by Basque critics and readers. I have selected ten poems by each author, and although I have not attempted to seek a balance of themes or poetic styles, I have tried not to exceed a limit of fifteen pages for each, and this is the reason why in some cases I have chosen fewer than ten poems. A brief biographical note accompanies each selection of poems. In the following pages, I will attempt to introduce the poems in the selection and locate them within each author's poetic development.

1975 was the year Franco died – a defining event: as I said earlier, after his death the new democratic government made Basque an official language and provided grants for publishing books in Basque. 1975 was also the year Gabriel Aresti died. Some of his translations, along with his translation of Eliot's *Four Quartets*, were published posthumously in a volume entitled *T. S. Eliot euskaraz* (Hordago,

1983). This volume also contained translations by two other authors: Joseba Sarrionandia and Jon Juaristi, both of whom (together with Bernardo Atxaga, Ruper Ordorika and Joxemari Iturralde) were part of the group POTT (meaning "failure"), which was created in Bilbao in 1978. This group adapted the provocative and innovative attitude of the avant-garde movements of the early twentieth century, especially the Dadaists. POTT defended the autonomy of literature, an autonomy that, as Bürger wrote (with regard to the avant-garde and the autonomy of art), did not seek to isolate literature from the rest of society, but the very opposite. The writers who formed POTT defined themselves as heirs of the Modernist masters. References to Borges, Kafka, Pound or Eliot abounded in *Pott,* the magazine the group published in the years 1978-1980. In the wake of POTT, poetry, short stories and other "short" genres went through a process of renewal and reached their heyday in the 1980s, a heyday was largely brought about by the many literary magazines that sprang up around the time, which acted as launching platforms for these new authors.

**BERNARDO ATXAGA** (b. 1951) has become the most internationally renowned Basque author thanks to his narrative works (especially books such as *Obabakoak* (Hutchinson, 1992) and *The Lone Man* (Harvill, 1996)), but he is also an exceptional poet. His works of poetry have received many awards and have been widely translated (see his biographical note) and he has also been a great influence in the evolution of contemporary Basque poetry. His poetry collection, *Etiopia*, was published by POTT in 1978 and took the literary establishment of the time by storm.

*Etiopia* could be defined as a collage of poems and stories with a circular structure. Two narratives open and close the book and in between, as in Dante's famous book, a Utopian journey to Ethiopia is laid out in nine circles of sand. In that sand the reader will find all the historical patrimony that forms the basis of Western culture. Thus Atxaga addresses the tedium brought about by the end of modernity, the impossibility of addressing poetic language itself, or what has been referred to as "the poetics of silence", which Mallarmé pioneered, and the impossibility of which was revealed by Wittgenstein's final assertion in his *Tractatus*. In *Etiopia,* Atxaga wants to revolutionise a poetic language saturated with rhetoric, and for this reason he announces that the silence-filled carriages arrive to join the fight against adjectives. There are ways to mock the sterility of language, to deny the Romantics' idealised assertions, and Atxaga borrows from the spirit of Dadaism and invokes it in the scattered "blah, blah, blahs" and "etceteras" of his poetry. He also includes references to comics, pop music, film or contemporary jingles in his poems. This is why we empathise with the lost protagonist in that labyrinthine city of expressionist and dramatic qualities. The poet's travelling companions are Nerval, Rigaut, Rimbaud and Cravan, who also tried to escape from the finality of the city, of language. *Etiopia* is characterised by savage irony, tenderness and the desire to break away from the poetry of the modernist tradition.

With the years, Atxaga's poetry became more "original" in Chesterton's sense of the word: it began to seek the origins of things. Freed from the baroque and far removed from the dramatics of his previous work, Atxaga, in *Poemas & Híbridos* (1990), tries to recover poetry's essence. For this purpose, he tears up the non-neutral, topical language that is traditionally used in poetry and mixes it with Dadaist strategies, with the primitive and the infantile. From then on, love and tenderness reign in the author's universe; but more importantly, he feels the need to distance himself from any sort of elitist conception about poetry-making and from pompous, affected poetry by introducing humour – or, as Barthes would say, the *gag*.[9] This use of humour made the poems in *Poemas & híbridos* less dramatic. The use of the first person extends to his poems, and he makes use of literary devices such as parallelism and repetition, both of which are widely used in the poetry of oral tradition and in song. The poetry of *Poemas & híbridos* is sensitive and natural; it is close to song, wants to recover an innocent way of looking at the world. This is precisely what the poem 'The Tale of the Hedgehog' offers us, whereas in poems such as 'Silly Song', humanity's inevitable tragic end is transformed through humour.

His collaboration with singers such as Ruper Ordorika, Mikel Laboa and Javier Muguruza, or with artists like Jose Luis Zumeta and Vicente Ameztoy translate into ground-breaking poetic ideas such as *Nueva Etiopía* (1996), a book in which the theme of Paradise starts to appear (in 'Finnish Day'). From then on, this theme becomes a constant in Atxaga's writing and has been positively central in the past few years (see his latest novel, *The Son of the Accordion Player*[10]). The theme of Paradise in Atxaga's works normally carries with it an anti-Utopian message. The poet prefers real life, a life full of joy and sadness because, as Brecht's well-known poem 'Don't let them fool you' says, there is nothing but life, and to lose it would be to lose everything. It is for this reason that the hitherto unpublished poems in this anthology repeat the word "life" in their paratext: life understood as something infinitely richer than its outcomes, or the joys or sorrows of its protagonists (see 'Life is Life'); exuberant life experi-

[9] Atxaga, B., *Alfabeto sobre la literatura infantil* (Valencia: Media Vaca, 1999), p. 63: "Barthes once said that the *gag*, the humorous element, freed the poem from its poetic mania, or in other words, from its need to strive for effect, its sickly sweet, pompous excesses."
[10] See Amaia Gabantxo's review in *The Times Literary Supplement*, no. 5289, 13 August, 2004.

enced through all the senses (see 'The Days go by'). Life, in the final analysis, is a path that must be enjoyed before it is too late (see 'Elegy'), a path towards the inevitable (see 'Death and the Zebras'). And thus the reader becomes the surprised witness of the frantic galloping of those zebras headed for a rather unexpected ending, or succumbs to the display of the products of nature in that stroll through a market – a stroll that will immerse the reader in a bucolic scene inhabited by happy peasants. Sensually overwhelmed by the market produce, the poet daydreams about scenes in the writings of Fray Luis de Granada, a sixteenth-century Spanish writer who was able to see greatness in small things, and about Francis Jammes, the rustic poet Rilke would have liked to be, who praised the pleasures of the humble life. Because, as Goethe wrote in his 1833 autobiography, *Poetry and Truth*, "life is good, in whatever form".

The career of another member of POTT, **JOSEBA SARRIONANDIA** (b. 1958), also included in this anthology, encompasses fiction, essays, children's and young people's literature, hybrid texts that subvert the boundaries between essay and fiction and, of course, poetry. He has published five volumes of poetry in total. He has translated poets like Coleridge, Eliot and Pessoa into Basque (see his biographical note). His literary obsessions have been recorded in books such as *Izkiriaturik aurkitu ditudan ene poemak* (My Poems that I found Already Written, 1985), which include translations of several poems as well as apocryphal ones. In his collection *Izuen gordelekuetan barrena* (In the Recesses of Fear, 1981) he deals with, among others, the themes of journeys and exile. The poem 'Nautical Logbook' opens this volume with a meditation on journeys whose final destination is exile, as we can see in 'Return Home'. There are echoes of Kavafis, Pessoa, Yeats, Dylan Thomas and Kafka in Sarrionandia's poetry, a poetry often inhabited by quotes and cultural references. Sarrionandia wrote in the prologue to *Izuen gordelekuetan barrena* that all literature is, in the final analysis, metaliterature. After the death of God and the death of the Author, the appropriation of the texts of others, the voices of others, become essential to the postmodern age. The stylistic richness, the musicality of the poems and the variety of the images and figures the poet uses (such as the labyrinth or the Ancient Mariner) are some of the most striking elements of his work. *Marinel zaharrak* (Ancient Mariners, 1987) contains a selection of poems from his previous collection, mixed in with a series of poems written in prison and later, after his escape.[11] The voice that speaks in this collection is pessimistic, disenchanted. Here the cultural refer-

---

[11] Sarrionandia was imprisoned in 1980 as a result of his involvement with ETA – he was condemned to 18 years in jail. He escaped in 1985, hidden inside a sound system speaker after a concert.

ences of the earlier work disappear and instead, the reader finds a marked ambivalence towards the power of literature (see 'Literature and Revolution'). A prisoner is forever condemned (see 'The Ex-Prisoner's Mind'), and for this reason Sarrionandia identifies with poets such as Mayakovsky and Villon, who also spent time in prison. He has said that, more and more, for him, writing poetry means desolation: "I hope that damaged poetry responds to damaged life and helps us look at our inner world, to discern the unknown, to seek a more truthful language. I think illiteracy is a more dignified option than the so-called poetry that loves artifice and showiness and rhymes 'amour' with 'toujours'."[12]

*Hnuy illa nyha majah yahoo (1985-1995)* is the meaningful title of Sarrionandia's latest volume of poems – a line taken from Jonathan Swift's *Gulliver's Travels*, which means "take care of thyself". As well as dealing with the theme of death, which is a constant in this poet's work, the volume is concerned mainly with exile. The book is split into ten parts that contain poems and short stories on a variety of subjects such as "the death of the hero, exile, the ancient mariner as memory, hope and rebellion, childhood, the country of the past and the imaginary future of the country... and the theme of love".[13] The T. S. Eliot quote on its opening page "Time present and time past / Are both perhaps present in time future" is taken from the first of the *Four Quartets* and suggests the destabil-isation of the idea of progress or time. This same idea is put forward by the short story that opens the book, which mixes past, present and future. In addition, the book includes poems from the author's previous works, which are not presented chronologically. The poet Kirmen Uribe, paraphrasing Frederic Jameson's ideas on the spatialisation of time in postmodernity, asserts that Sarrionandia's poetry reflects on the ubiquitous, and therefore spatial, present which the rupture with temporal continuity has condemned us to.[14] Exile, childhood as a lost (Utopian) paradise and even the heterotopias that appear in some of his works, like the novel *Lagun Izoztua* (The Frozen Friend, 2001), make up the spatial corpus of Sarrionandia's literary universe.

In *Hnuy illa nyha majah yahoo* the poet uses the first-person plural to state that we will always be exiled, that to return home is absolutely impossible, because home – the motherland we knew and wished for – does not exist (see 'The Minotaur speaks'). And thus,

---

[12] See Parreño, J. M. & Gallero, J. L., *8 poetas raros* (Madrid: Ardora, 1992), pp. 216-217.
[13] Otaegi, L., 2007, 'XXth Century Basque Poetry', in Olaziregi, M. J. (Ed.), *History of Basque Literature*, (Reno: University of Nevada Press (due for publication in 2007).
[14] See Uribe, K., 1998, 'Asalto a los cielos. Estética y escritura en la poesía de Atxaga y Sarrionandia', *Insula* 623, pp. 23-25.

whereas return is impossible for this poet, true poetry is possible, despite the fact that it still remains to be written (see 'Poetic Proposal').

**FELIPE JUARISTI** (b. 1957) has written twenty books. He is very active in cultural circles, having edited literary magazines, collaborated with publishing houses, written prologues for books, and so on. He has also translated authors such as Maupassant, Wilde, Zimnik, Futrelle, Breytenbach, Grossman, Celaya, Mirande, Aramburu and Otxoa. Nowadays, he writes columns and reviews for several newspapers and has received numerous awards – the Euskadi Prize twice, first in 1998 for the poetry collection *Galderen geografia* (The Geography of Questions) and in 2000 for his book for young people *Animalien iñauteria* (Animal Carnival), and also the Rosalía de Castro Prize in 2002 for his literary career (awarded to him by Galician PEN). As the critic Iñaki Aldekoa[15] has said, Juaristi's poetic temperament is indebted to the poetic, expressive and sentimental imaginary world of symbolism, to the *fin de siècle* movement. The Romantic tradition of authors such Hölderlin or Keats, Schopenhauer's thought and the sensuality of Klimt's paintings are part of that imaginary world. It therefore seems natural that his first collection of poems *Denbora, nostalgia* (Time, Nostalgia, 1984), which received the Spanish Critics' Prize in 1986, should concern the tension between memory and the irreversible passing of time. It is significant that in his prologue, Juaristi echoes John Milton's definition of poetry, saying that poetry must be "simple, sensual and ardent" and indeed, in his poems we see eroticisim, passion and sensuality. It is worth noting that the book is peppered with illustrations. These portray everyday scenes and reflect the abandonment the protagonist feels: an absence, the emptiness someone has left behind. The constant dialogue between East and West, metaphysics and poetry, the passionate past and the painful present, are at the core of the first poem in his selection ('It makes no difference...'). Juaristi's second book, *Hiriaren melankolia* (City Melancholy, 1986), revisits his previous volume's poetic tone and again is full of sensuous images and musical verses. In this collection the poet moves from the plenitude of desire to its impossibility, and again mourns the fact that words, language, are wounded "because their wings are broken" (see 'Smoothy').

In 1993 Juaristi published *Laino artean zelatari* (Sentinel in the Mist), a collection of longer poems of great musicality. The prevalent concern here is more philosophical than in earlier works, more reflective. His key concern here is man – humanity. In this regard Juaristi has invoked the spirit of Cernuda in saying that "we can only know

---

[15] In Aldekoa, I., 'Felipe Juaristi', *Thélème,* vol. 17 (2002), p. 63.

poetry through man".[16] In Juaristi's view, we can only know our-
selves if we look within (see 'Metropolis 2') because, as the poem
'Niaren, geografia' (The Geography of the "I") from *Laino artean
zelatari* says, the "I" can only be found in the remotest depths of
ourselves, like the treasures ancient galleons used to carry. The poet
knows that words – those internalised words he is trying to eluci-
date,[17] – are not good travelling companions because they are worn
(see 'The Isthmus of Panama'). Our experience of modernity has
confirmed that this suspicious attitude towards words has eventually
turned into a mistrust of the key ideas and concepts of Western thought
(see 'Vanity of Vanities'). The protagonist of *Laino artean zelatari*
experiences that lack of trust in language with detachment, because
he knows himself to be accompanied, filled with infinite echoes, voices
and personae (see 'Nevsky Prospect').

A geography plagued with questions asked in alphabetical order,
and briefer, more concise writing are the characteristics of Juaristi's
next book, *Galderen geografia* (The Geography of Questions, 1998).
The poet, knowing that poetry cannot alter time or affect the world,
persists in his belief in what poetry should be: a contributor to the
moral regeneration of society.[18] For this reason he reminds us of
immeasurable tragedies, so that they are never forgotten (see
'Auschwitz'), or sketches out the politically conflictive geography of
the Basque Country to speak of the suffering it has created (see
'Geography'). Like Socrates, the poet persists in his questions about
essential dichotomies such as Life and Death, Fire and Ice, Ques-
tions and Answers. Because he is a man, and not a poet-prophet in
possession of the Truth, all he is doing is reaching out a questioning
hand – because he knows how to appreciate the great insignificant
moments of life, and can offer up his *locus amoenus*, his fertile gar-
den full of pleasurable, dream-inducing fruits ('Gardener'). The last
poem in the selection, "Rembrandt wants to paint infinity...", belongs
to his last collection, *Begi-ikarak* (Eye Tremors, 2004), which re-
ceived the Spanish Critics' Prize in 2005. Again philosophy and po-
etry, ethics and aesthetics walk hand in hand in a collection whose
dominant themes are the experience of life and the exploration of
pain ("for in the end, man / is an animal that drags solitude and pain").
The literary critic Lourdes Otaegi has put it succinctly: "Most impor-
tant are the three poems dedicated to Rembrandt, who wanted to
paint infinity. These are the rings of the cycle that lend the book its
structure, and through them the poet expresses the human desire to

---

[16] In Juaristi, F. *et al.*, *¿Qué puede la poesía?*, (Bassarai: Vitoria-Gasteiz, 2002), p. 15.
[17] *Ibid.*, p. 15
[18] *Ibid.*, p. 16.

be bird, to be light and infinity, and the pain experienced by the impossibility of it all."[19]

The next three poets – Rikardo Arregi, Miren Agur Meabe and Kirmen Uribe – were first published in the 1990s.

**RIKARDO ARREGI DIAZ DE HEREDIA** (b. 1958) is one of the most persuasive poetic voices of the 1990s. He has translated poems by Wislawa Szymborska, Sophia de Melo, Eugénio Andrade and Ernestina de Champourcin amongst others. He has published two collections: *Hari hauskorrak* (Fragile Threads, 1993) and *Kartografia* (Cartography, 1998), both of which have received the Spanish Critics' Prize.

For Arregi, poetry is the product of the continuous pull between the desire to express something and the inability to express it; in other words, it is a constant fight with / against language.[20] Eliot wrote that every poetic revolution is, deep down, a revolution of language. It is precisely for this reason that poets throughout the ages have fought against the tyranny of words. Arregi has been known to quote Auden's assertion that it is necessary to detoxify words to explain one's position.[21] For Arregi, poetry is more than a game, more than a literary artefact; for him, it must be able to say (or show) the cracks and underbelly of what we call reality. His first collection could be described as "cultured", "Hellenic" or "classical". The voices of Kavafis, Pessoa and Auden echo throughout *Hari hauskorrak*. His, as Iñaki Aldekoa said, is the voice of a poet who understands art and history. His literary imagination is informed by a love of Hellenism, antiquity and the Arab world, and his poems on the sensuous enjoyment of life take place against the backdrop of this antiquity.[22]

His second book, *Kartografia*, confirm his status. This collection is a cartography of the author's poetic universe, one that – as the Sarrionandia quote in the volume's second section indicates – shows some parts of his universe and hides others. The parts he shows are there to root the thematic axis of his previous work: again, he writes about desire and pleasure, about the pre-occupation with the passing of time; he reiterates that to journey (to love) is what matters, and not the end of the journey; he insists that remembrance, memory, are constructed and have nothing to do with the past. As the first poem of

---

[19] Otaegi, L., 2007, *op. cit.* p. 275.

[20] See Arregi, R., 'Poetika', in Arregi, R. *et al.*, *Poetikak & Poemak* (Donostia: Erein, 2005), p. 27.

[21] Contemporary authors such as Margaret Atwood have made similar assertions: "For me poetry is where the language is renewed" (in Geddes, G. (Ed.), 1996, *20th Century Poetry & Poetics*, Oxford University Press, 1996, p. 785). Arregi quotes Atwood and others (Carson, Bachmann, González Iglesias, Portela, Lopo, *et al.*) as poets whose love of poetry he has found affecting (in Arregi, *et al.*, 2005, *op cit.*, p. 26).

[22] Aldekoa, I., *Historia de la Literatura Vasca*, (Donostia: Erein, 2004), p. 243.

his in this anthology ('Papers on the Pavement') says: "and as from now / memories here from the future." As with Sarrionandia's poetry, here past, present and future are fused in a poetry that states, as Eliot did, that "all time is unredeemable" (see *Four Quartets*). The spatialisation of time, a characteristic I have already mentioned with regard to Sarrionandia, implies that the subject's temporality has been destroyed. In other words, the subject can no longer be defined as a unified individual in a temporal continuum, and thus can only place himself in a space which, as Jameson has said, has become global in late capitalism.[23] It is for this reason that, in *Kartografia*, Arregi draws a map that includes places as obscure as San Blas (Nayarit), the Basque Country or Ireland, and even heterotopias such as spas, Saint Alexander Nevsky's cathedral in Sophia, and territories built on literary texts (see 'The Sleeping Land III'). Other poems, like 'Onassis Tavern', deny that the past was a better place, thus refusing to bow to the classical world. In the excellent poem '66 Lines from the City under Siege', a divided self denounces the cruelty of the siege of Sarajevo. The journey the poet makes around his native city, Gasteiz, becomes a virtual itinerary around the Yugoslav city. As we go deeper into *Kartografia*, the map Arregi sketches out shows us cities that, far from being the cosmopolitan centres of the modern age, are closer to those described by Calvino in *Invisible Cities*, because they are made up by, among others, desire, violence, forgetfulness and literature. Above all, the poet reminds us that, like Calvino's city of Cecilia, the city is everywhere and as a result, "nothing is new, nothing old" under the same moon (see 'The Moon Anywhere'). Other territories of Arregi's poetic landscape are related to music, populated by poems composed to the beats of boleros, arias or Lieder, as is the case in 'The Territories of Music II'. The last chapter of *Kartografia*, 'The Seas I see', introduces subjects and a voice closer to the mundane: a reality, as reflected in the poem 'Telephone Promises', that knows a lot about difficulties and frustrations. The two other poems that complete the selection of his poems are more recent and concern desire and drive (see 'Love Poem I'), or parody Gilen of Aquitaine's Canto IV – 'Farai un vers de dreit nien' – a very modern poem about nothing (see 'Like Gilen of Aquitaine').

**MIREN AGUR MEABE** (b. 1962) started her literary career with a collection of short stories, *Uneka... Gaba* (Momentarily... Night, 1986). She has also published a number of books for children and young people, among them *Itsaslabarreko etxea* (The Cliff House, 1999), which received the Euskadi Prize for young people's literature. This is a gothic adventure story, lyrical in tone, which is strongly

[23] Jameson, Frederic 'Postmodernism, or the cultural logic of late capitalism', *New Left Review*, 146 (1984), pp. 53-92.

influenced by one of the author's favourite novels, *Jane Eyre*. But it is her poetry which has received most critical acclaim; her first collection was *Oi, hondarrezko emakaitz!* (Oh, Wild Woman of Sand!, 1999), but her greatest success was *Azalaren Kodea* (The Code of the Skin, 2000), which received the Spanish Critics' Prize in the year of its publication. Meabe has said that rebellion, non-conformity and a critique of stereotypes are at the heart of this book.[24] The titles of the four different sections that make up the volume ('Notes', 'Scars', 'Tattoos' and 'Passwords') reveal the author's demand for a new code of communication, one that is more personal and ambiguous, more body-centred – a code unrelated to words, a code of the skin (see 'The Code'). Love, observed from different perspectives (nostalgia for lost love, desire and eroticism, the pain of distance) is an ever-present theme, but there is room for other subjects too, such as the stress of everyday life, solidarity with the oppressed (see 'Brief Notes (1)'), and the rejection of aesthetic clichés. Meabe's poetry loves the concrete (see 'Concrete Things'), the small but great actions that fill the day-to-day lives of contemporary women. In a constant game of references to non-verbal codes, Meabe's poetry bursts through the page from the margins, to reclaim a new female voice through a game of oneiric references and sensuous images. The poet, in other words, seeks to find a form of expression that deliberately steps away from standard language, which is insufficient. In the chapter entitled 'Scars', bodily descriptions give way to sweet sexual beckonings in which the tongue, saliva, fruits and animals become sustenance for oneiric fantasies about sexual encounters (see "Scoop the pale flow…"). From this perspective, it could be said that Meabe's poetry moves along the poetic lines established by other Spanish female poets of the 1990s which, according to Shannon Keefe Ugalde, could be described as a poetics that leaves aside the idea of the abandoned woman and chooses instead to represent desire and erotic ecstasy openly.[25] Meabe's style is direct, emotive, rich in imagery, and possesses an undeniable lyrical power. The poet has expressed her alliance to the poetry of experience as it is understood in the Iberian literary context.[26] Her poetry could be seen as a continuation of the legacy established by other Basque female poets of the 1970s, such as Amaia Lasa and Arantxa Urretabizkaia, whose writing was close to the French feminism of difference and whose aim was to decon-

---

[24] Urkiza, A., *Zortzi unibertso, zortzi idazle,* (Irun: Alberdania, 2006), p. 274.
[25] Keefe Ugalde, S., 'Los grandes temas: ellas también', *Zurgai*, July 2004, pp. 6-17.
[26] When asked which school of poetry she identifies with most, Miren Agur Meabe answers: "The poetry of experience, especially because it poeticises aspects, anecdotes, of everyday life. This poetry is clear and intense, and drinks from reality while still leaving room for digression and wonderment." (in Urkiza, A., 2006, *op. cit.,* p. 354).

struct images of femininity through new ways of verbalising and expressing the female self. Some of her most recent poems included in this anthology deal with the loss of a loved one (see 'The Ant II'), and, again, with the oneiric life of unexpressed – and perhaps unexpressable – love (see 'Aeolia' or 'Water Dreams III').

**KIRMEN URIBE** (b. 1970) has written poems, short stories, children's and young people's literature, essays and plays. He is renowned for his essay writing as well as his poetry, and two of his essays have been awarded the Becerro de Bengoa Prize: 'Lizardi eta erotismoa' (Lizardi and eroticism, which he co-wrote with Jon Elordi, published in 1996), and 'Zazpi saio, zazpi lehio' (Seven Essays, Seven Windows, unpublished). He has translated authors such as Raymond Carver, Sylvia Plath, Wislawa Szymborska and Mahmud Darwish into Basque, and has taken part in several multimedia projects integrating music and visual arts as well as poetry (like *Bar Puerto*, 2001, and *Zaharregia, txikiegia agian,*[27] 2003). He received the Spanish Critics' Prize in 2003 for his first collection, *Bitartean heldu eskutik* (2001); the book was enthusiastically received in the Basque Country and internationally – it has been translated into Spanish, French and English.[28] Uribe has stated that he is mistrustful of words, especially of words written with capital letters[29] because, as he writes in 'The Unsayable': "Floods have washed away the bridge between words and things." This mistrust of language takes us back to the crisis of representation brought about by the end of modernity. In Uribe's poetry, the solutions to this problem are postmodern. Thus, although everything has already been said it merits repetition – "But still, I confess that when I hear you / say 'my love' I feel electric, / be it truth, be it lie" – and there are other languages available, such as the language of the body. Hence the title of his collection: when language fails to communicate, a gesture is a better option – like taking a loved one's hand ("hold my hand awhile"). In this work Uribe presents a variety of personae, a concerto of voices that enact the dissolution of the subject and its fragmentation into thousands of particles.

Paraphrasing Wallace Stevens, Uribe has stated that a poem must be like a revelation of nature, a revelation that has its origins in emotion.[30]

---

[27] *Too Old, Too Small, Maybe* toured the USA in 2003 with Kirmen Uribe and musicians Bingen Mendizabal and Rafa Rueda and New York poet-translator Elizabeth Macklin.

[28] Translated by Elizabeth Macklin as *Meanwhile Take My Hand* (USA: Graywolf Press, 2007), it has received excellent reviews (see www.graywolf.org).

[29] Uribe, K., 'Ez dakit' in Arregi, R. *et al.*, *Poetikak & Poemak* (Erein, 2005), p. 144.

[30] Uribe, K., *op. cit.*, p. 150. As regards emotions, a review published in *Los Angeles Times Review* is particularly revealing. The critic describes the emotional effect of Uribe's poems thus: "The poems are a beacon of light and memory, surrounded by conflict, explosion and interruption."

Poets such as Sandburg, Bachmann, Plath, Atwood, Herbert, Arregi, Atxaga and Sarrionandia are some of Uribe's influences in this collection, which avoids rhetorical language, instead seeking freshness and simplicity. The critic Ezkerra has described the book as follows:

> This collection has seven sections, each dealing with a separate theme. The poet reflects on technology, progress and the search for perfection, and their negative impact on contemporary society or himself, and the need to return to essential things. As one of the poems states, their objective is "to adapt the human being to the measure of the world." [31]

It could be said that these poems try to implicate the reader by presenting fragments of reality in plain, direct language. These are poems that speak of silent, hidden sorrows that can suddenly break through the apparent calmness of a normal day (see 'The River'), or of the joy of two naked bodies (see 'The Island'). But most revealing is the humane aspect of his work, his solidarity with the more marginalized elements of society. He writes of illegal immigrants that arrive in Spain from North Africa with "hands wet with orange juice" (see 'Mahmud'), whose dreams are more often than not torn apart; or of dying drug addicts whose last request is a gesture of love (see 'The Visit'). The poet also revisits his fear of perfection (see 'Perfect Things') and rummages through his childhood memories to reflect on the chasm between nature and culture (see 'The Cuckoo') or to assert that life is an adventure that should be lived to the full (see 'Way Beyond'). Uribe's collection is bursting with life; or, to put it in Rikardo Arregi's words in the prologue to *Bitartean heldu eskutik*: "This book is alive, that's all." [32]

Life, that word which has cropped up so often in this introduction, beckons again. Poetry always brings us back to it: as Wislawa Szymborska has said, you cannot talk exclusively about poetry because at some point life takes over again. Indeed, Basque life, and poetry, is what this anthology is about and as Walter Benjamin would have said, they have found new life in English translation.

*Mari Jose Olaziregi,*
*University of the Basque Country*

---

[31] See http://www.basqueliterature.com/katalogoak/egileak/uribe
[32] Arregi, R., 2001, 'Zubiak', in Uribe, K., *Bitartean heldu eskutik* (Susa, 2001), p. 10.

This anthology, the first of its kind, has been a long time in the making. Perhaps it already started happening before its inception – maybe that summer day in 1999 when, shortly before starting my MA in Literary Translation at the University of East Anglia, I bought eighteen volumes of Basque poetry in a bookshop in Bilbao. No Basque poetry had ever been translated directly into English at that time, and my perhaps somewhat naïve intention then was to get people to think of poetry when they thought of the Basque Country, and not of terrorism, as is now sadly the case. Tragic and unsolved as that aspect of Basque life may be, it doesn't define how Basque people are, how they view the world, how they approach it. There may be, as they say, "something in the water", something that predisposes Basques to song and poetry. Hopefully, in reading this anthology, you will be able to get a sense of that.

Translating poetry isn't easy work, but it is beautiful work, if one loves language and its possibilities. It is not my aim to be a faithful translator, in the sense of seeking equivalencies or lexical parallels. I like to say that I try not to be too beleaguered by the meaning of the original work. Rather, I try to replicate what the original work *does*. This process isn't necessarily logical.

Because Basque is an agglutinative language (meaning that all prepositions, adverbs and articles hook onto the end of nouns), each word on the page is a bundle of meaning. It is a good language for poetry. Agglutination allows for brilliant internal rhymes and rich rhythmical patterns, and produces intensely synthetic poems. Fortunately, English is an extremely flexible language that lends itself to synthesis, to compressed sentences infused with meaning. This makes my work much easier.

The other thing I look for is how a poem makes its impact. This is a very subjective exercise. More often than not, this impact can't be replicated by just translating the line's lexical meaning. And this is where the illogical work starts. It's a little like when, as children, my friends and I played shopkeepers in the playground and gave three leaves in exchange for a stone, or a fistful of sand for a piece of broken glass. There is no saying how the brain works out the permutations: a solitary "here" in exchange for four internally rhymed "ki / ik" sounds, which is what I came up with for a line in Rikardo Arregi's 'Papers on the Pavement'. In Basque, the line read "etorkizunetik datozkigu engoitik / oroitzapenak" – meaning, literally, "from now on they come to us from the future / memories". To my ear, these sounds capture the mind's attention; they are the hooks in the fishing line. The first "ik" is a temporal preposition and the last a temporal adverb; the second "ki" is in the middle of a verb that is used both temporally and spatially (to come) and echoes the "ki" in "etor*ki*zunetik" ("etorkizun" means future). These sounds pin the notions of time and space to this line. And for me, they have a physicality that demands to be expressed in the English version too. "As for now / memories *here* from the future" was my answer: that sonorous and slightly awkward "here" was my hook. These are the exchanges of twigs for pebbles that I am referring to.

I would like to thank the authors for entrusting their poems to my care. I would also like to thank the library of Babel for all the lines, words and ideas stolen or retrieved from its shelves. Thank you also to the Wingate Foundation, for helping when help was most needed. I am also grateful to Peter Holm-Jensen, Daniel Kane, Nathan Hamilton, Jennifer Oey, Peter Bush, Betsy Rosenberg and Margaret Jull Costa, all of whom read these poems at different stages and offered clever insights. Thank you, Marijo, for the friendship and the belief.

*Amaia Gabantxo*

# BERNARDO   ATXAGA

## SIX POEMS, TWO SONGS
### SEI POEMA, BI KANTU

PHOTO: GORKA SALMERON

BERNARDO ATXAGA (JOSE IRAZU) was born in Asteasu, Gipuzkoa, in 1951, and belongs to the group of Basque writers who began publishing in their mother tongue, Euskera, in the 1970s. He graduated in economics from the University of the Basque Country and later studied philosophy at Barcelona University.

His first short story, *Ziutateaz*, was published in 1976 and his first poetry collection, *Etiopia*, in 1978. Both works received the Spanish Critics' Prize for the best works in their categories in the Basque language.

He writes in most genres: poetry, short stories, novels, essays and more. National – and international – recognition followed the publication of *Obabakoak*, which was awarded the Spanish Premio Nacional de Narrativa in 1989.

*Obabakoak* has been translated into more than twenty-five languages. The novels *The Lone Man, The Lone Woman* and *Two Brothers* have been translated into English, and his latest novel, *The Son of the Accordion Player*, appears in English from Harvill Press in 2007.

His poetry collection, *Etiopia* (its Spanish title is *Poemas & Híbridos*), has been translated into French, Finnish and Italian, the latter receiving the Cesare Pavese Prize. Translations of many of his poems and short stories have been published in prestigious magazines throughout Europe and the Americas.

**SEI POEMA**

**TRIKUARENA**

Esnatu da trikua habi hosto lehorrez egindakoan,
eta dakizkien hitz guztiak ekartzen ditu gogora;
gutxi gora behera, aditzak barne, hogeita zazpi hitz.

Eta gero pentsatzen du: amaitu da negua,
Ni trikua naiz, Bi zapelatz gora dabiltza hegaletan;
Barraskilo, Zizare, Zomorro, Armiarma, Igel,
Zein putzu edo zulotan ezkutatzen zarete?
Hor dago erreka, Hau da nire erresuma, Goseak nago.

Eta berriro dio: hau da nire erresuma, Goseak nago,
Barraskilo, Zizare, Zomorro, Armiarma, Igel,
Zein putzu edo zulotan ezkutatzen zarete?

Ordea bertan gelditzen da bera ere hosto lehor balitz,
artean ez baita eguerdia baino, lege zahar batek
galarazi egiten baitizkio eguzkia, zerua eta zapelatzak

Baina gaua dator, joan dira zapelatzak, eta trikuak,
Barraskilo, Zizare, Zomorro, Armiarma, Igel,
Erreka utzi eta mendiaren pendizari ekiten dio,
bere arantzetan seguru nola egon baitzitekeen
Gerlari bat bere ezkutuaz, Espartan edo Corinton;
Eta bat-batean, zeharkatu egiten du
belardiaren eta kamio berriaren arteko muga,
Zure eta nire denboran sartzen da pauso bakar batez;
Eta nola bere hiztegi unibertsala ez den
azkeneko zazpi mila urteotan berritu,
ez ditu ezagutzen gure automobilaren argiak,
ez da ohartzen bere heriotzaren hurbiltasunaz ere.

## SIX POEMS

### THE TALE OF THE HEDGEHOG

The hedgehog wakes up in his nest of dry leaves
his mind suddenly filled with all the words he knows.
Counting the words, including the verbs, more or less, they come to
                                        twenty-seven.

Later he thinks: the winter is over,
I'm a hedgehog, up fly two eagles, high up,
Snail, Worm, Insect, Spider, Frog,
which ponds or holes are you hiding in?
There is the river, this is my kingdom, I am hungry.

And he repeats: this is my kingdom, I am hungry,
Snail, Worm, Insect, Spider, Frog,
which ponds or holes are you hiding in?

But he remains still like a dry leaf,
because it's just midday and an old law
forbids him sun, sky and eagles.

But when night comes, gone are the eagles; and the hedgehog,
Snail, Worm, Insect, Spider, Frog,
disregards the river, attends to the steepness of the mountain,
as sure of his spines as a warrior
in Sparta or Corinth could have been of his shield;
suddenly, he crosses the boundary
between the meadow and the new road
with a single step that takes him right into my and your time.
And given that his universal vocabulary has not been renewed
in the last seven thousand years,
he doesn't understand our car lights
or see his death coming.

**ADAN ETA BIZITZA**

Gaixotu zen Adan paradisua utzi eta aurreneko neguan,
eta eztulka, buruko minez, hogeita hemeretziko sukarraz,
negarrari eman zion Magdalenak gerora emango bezala,
eta Evagana zuzenduz "hil egingo naiz" esan zion oihuka,
"gaizki nago, maite, hilurren, ez dakit zer gertatzen zaidan".

Harritu egin zen Eva hitz haiekin, *hil, hilurren, gaizki, maite,*
eta berriak iruditu zitzaizkion, hizkuntza arrotz batekoak,
eta ezpain artean ibili zituen maiz, *hil, hilurren, gaizki, maite,*
harik eta zehazki ulertzen zituela iruditu zitzaion unea arte.
Ordurako sendatua zegoen Adan, eta poz pozik zebilen.

Paradisuaz geroko lehen gertaera hark segida luzea izan zuen,
eta lehengoez gain, *hil, hilurren, gaizki, maite,* Adan zein Evak
hitz berriak ikasi behar izan zituzten, *min, lan, bakardade, poz*
eta beste hamaika, *denbora, neke, algara, eder, ikara, kemen*;
hiztegia hazten zenarekin batera, zimurtuz joan zitzaien azala.

Zahartu zen erabat Adan, sentitu zuen hurbil heriotzaren ordua,
eta Evarekin elkarrizketa sakon bat izateko gogoa sortu zitzaion;
"Eva", esan zion, "ez zen ezbehar bat izan paradisuaren galtzea;
oinazeak oinaze, minak min, gure Abelen zoritxarra halako zoritxar,
bizi izan duguna izan da, zentzurik nobleenean esanda, bizitza".

Adanen hilobi atarian malko arruntak isuri ziren, gatz eta urezkoak,
lurrera erortzerakoan hiazinto edo arrosa alerik eman ez zutenak,
eta Kain izan zen, paradoxaz, negarrez bortitzen puskatu zena;
Gero Evak irribarre xamurrez gogoratu zuen Adanen lehen gripea
eta halaxe, lasai, etxera joan eta salda beroa hartu zuten, eta txokolatea.

**ADAM AND LIFE**

The winter after leaving Paradise Adam got sick;
he had a cough, a headache, thirty-nine-degree fever,
and cried like Mary Magdalene would all those years later.
Coming to Eve he shouted "I'm going to die I'm so unwell
my love, I'm in agony, I don't know what's wrong with me."

Eve was surprised by those words *die, agony, unwell, my love,*
they seemed new like they belonged to a foreign tongue,
so she rolled them over in her mouth *die, agony, unwell, my love,*
until one day she was certain she understood them completely.
By then Adam had recovered and was as happy as anything.

After leaving Paradise lots of other stuff happened
and on top of the old *die, agony, unwell, my love* both Adam and Eve
had to learn new words like *pain, work, loneliness, joy*
and more, such as *time, fatigue, laughter, beauty, fear, courage;*
as their dictionary grew, so did the number of wrinkles on their faces.

Adam was getting old, he sensed his time would soon be up
and felt the need to have a deep conversation with Eve;
"Eve," he said, "it wasn't such a misfortune to lose Paradise;
despite all the suffering, all the pain, despite what happened to Abel.
What we have lived through is, in the noblest sense of the word, life."

Ordinary tears were shed by Adam's grave, tears of salt and water,
no hyacinths or roses sprang up where they fell.
Funnily enough, it was Cain who who wept most bitterly.
Afterwards Eve smiled tenderly remembering Adam's first 'flu
and all soothed she went home, drank hot soup, ate chocolate.

**ELEGIA**

Gure izebak, eta gure ama maiteak berdin,
berandu ohartzen ziren bizitzaren garrantziaz,
hirurogeita hamar urterekin, edo laurogeiekin,
eta txoraturik aurkikuntza latz hura zela eta
nahastuta ibiltzen ziren hainbat hilabetez,
bere seme alabei bazkaririk prestatu gabe
supermerkatuan gauza xelebreak erosiz,
telefono dei amaigabeak nornahiri eginez;
etxe atarian ovni bat ikusi izan balute bezala.

Gero, denbora galdua eskuratu behar zutela eta,
gure izebak, eta gure ama maiteak berdin,
herriko udaletxeak antolatu gimnasia saioetarako
ematen zuten izena, "Urlia naiz, edo Sandia,
ez, ez dizut esango zenbat urte bete ditudan";
eta handik aurrera oihuka, korrika, jauzika,
ematen zioten hasiera egunari, bat-bi, bat-bi,
bat-bi eta txalo, bat-bi, bat-bi, bat-bi eta txalo.
Polikiroldegiak hozki jasotzen zizkien algarak

Ikasle larderiatsuaren aginduetara makurturik
oihuka, korrika, jauzika jotzen zuten aurrera,
eta aldian behin afari bat egiten zuten denek
txandala kendu eta soineko dotoreak jantziz;
egun batean, azkenez, sukaldean zorabiatu
eta zerraldo erortzen ziren semealaben oinetan,
eta hantxe gelditzen ziren hilda beraien kideek
polikiroldegian gimnasiari ekiten zioten bitartean,
bat-bi- bat-bi, bat-bi eta txalo, bat-bi, bat-bi.

**ZEBRAK ETA HERIOTZA**

Hogeita laua, hogeita bosta eta hogeita seia
Neramatzan aurrean, atzean hirurogeta bata
Hiruroigeita bia eta hirorogeita hirua,
Eta bat batean ehun eta hamazortziak
Ehun eta hemeretziak eta ehun eta hogeiak

## ELEGY

Our aunts, and our dear mothers too,
usually grasped the importance of life too late,
at the age of sixty, or eighty,
and faced with such a discovery, would lose their heads
and be confused for a month or two;
they'd forget their children's visits,
buy weird things at the supermarket,
and yell endlessly down the phone at everyone,
as if a UFO had landed on their doorstep.

Then, determined to make up for lost time,
our aunts and dear mothers too,
would sign up for the aerobics class
the council promoted at the local
sports centre: "I'm so-and-so, or whatever,
and no, I'd rather not say my age";
from then on they'd start the day
yelling, running, jumping, and-one-and-two and one-and-two,
and clap, and-one-and-two and one-and-two, and clap.
The sports hall was deaf to their laughter.

Following the orders of the tyrannical instructor
they yelled, ran, jumped and one-and-two-etc.
Sometimes they all had dinner together,
no track suits, smart clothes instead;
until one day, finally, they'd faint and fall
on the kitchen floor right at their children's feet,
and end their lives there, die, while their friends
yelled, ran, jumped at the sports centre:
and-one-and-two and one-and-two, and clap,
and-one-and-two and one-and-two, and clap.

## DEATH AND THE ZEBRAS

We were 157 zebras
galloping across the parched plain,
I ran behind zebra 24,
25 and 26,
ahead of 61 and 62
and suddenly we were overtaken with a jump
by 118 and 119,

Albotik aurretatu gintuzten ibaia, ibaia, ibaia,
Oihu eginez, ibaia, ibaia, ura, ibaia, ura,
Eta hogeitalaua, hogeitabosta eta hobeitaseia
Ibaia, ura, ibaia, ura oihuka hasi ziren, eta
Laurogeiak, laurogeita batak, laurogeita biak,
Aurrea hartu ziguten zalapartan ura ibaia,
Ura ibaia, ura, ura, ura, eta aurrera, aurrera,
Eta hogeitalauak ezkerrera egin zuen, eta
Hogeita bostak eta hogeita seiak eskubitara,
Eta eguzkia ikusi nuen ibaian, ura distiratsu,

Ibaia, eguzkia, ura, ura, ura, aurrera, aurrera,
Eta zazpiarekin eta zortziarekin gurutzatu nintzen,
Bustita zetozen, bustita urez, aho bete urez,
Eta aurrera, aurrera, bostarekin eta seiarekin
Gurutzatu nintzen, kokodriloak esan zuen seiak,
Eta aurrera, aurrera, kokodriloak, kokodriloak
Egin zuten berriro oihu seiak, eta gero bostak,
Eta hamarrak, hamazazpiak, hogeiak, denak oihu
Kokodriloak, kokodriloak, eta ura edan nuen,
ura edan nuen, ura, ura, ura, ur distiratsua,
Ura eguzkiz betea, *kokodriloak* egin zuen oihu
Nire ezkerrean hogeita lauak, *kokodriloak*, ura
Ur distiratsua, eta bustita, atera nintzen bustita,
Eta berrehun eta bostarekin eta berrehun eta biarekin
Gurutzatu nintzen ibaia, ibaia oihuka zetozen, ura,
Ura, ura, kokodrikoak esan nien, eta korrika segi nuen
Eta hogeitabosta eta hogeitaseia neramatzan aurrean,
atzean hirurogeta bata, iruroigeita bia, hirorogeita hirua,
eta korrika jarraitu nien, eta hogeitalauaren tokia
hartu nuen hogeitabostaren eta hogeitaseiaren ondoan.

both of them shouting *river, river,*
and 25, very happy, repeated *river, river,*
and suddenly 130 reached us
running, shouting, very happy, *river, river,*
and 25 took a left turn
ahead of 24 and 26
and suddenly I saw the sun on the river
sparkling full sparkly splashes
and 8 and 9 passed me
running in the opposite direction
with their mouths full of water
and wet legs and wet chests
very happy, shouting *go, go, go*
and I suddenly collided with 5 and 7
who were also running in the opposite direction
but shouting *crocodiles, crocodiles,*
and then 6 and 30 and 14 ran past us
very frightened, shouting, *crocodiles, crocodiles, go, go, go*
and I drank water, I drank sparkling water
full of sparkly splashes and sun
*crocodile, crocodile,* shouted 25, very frightened,
*crocodile,* I repeated, rearing back;
and running very frightened in the opposite direction
I suddenly collided with 149
and 150 and 151,
running, shouting, very happy, *river, river,*
*crocodiles, crocodiles*, I shouted back, very frightened
with my mouth full of water
and wet legs and wet chest.
I kept galloping across the parched plain
behind 24 and 26
ahead of 60 and 61
and suddenly I saw, suddenly I saw a gap
between 24 and 26, a gap
and I kept galloping across the parched plain
and I saw the gap again, the gap again,
between 24 and 26
and suddenly I jumped and filled the gap.

We were 149 zebras
galloping across the parched plain,
and ahead of me were 12, 13
and 14, and behind me
43 and 44.

**EGUNAK BA DOATZI**

Intxaur eta urrak ikusi genituen azokan zakuka saltzen,
eta baita ehiztariek botatako hegabera, uxo eta erbiak ere
txoko batean zintzilik, burutxoa bularrean eroria zeukatela.
Eta ziza txuriak tontorretan zeuden, eta mizpirak ere bai,
eta loreen sailean, krisantemoak ziren nagusi, eta lirioak.
"Tomaterik ez daukat, eta lekak ere banaka batzuk",
esan zigun nekazariak buruko painelua ondo kokatuz,
eta piperrak ere azkenekoak ziruditen, oso gutxi zeuden.
Itxi egin nituen begiak: erbiak basoan zebiltzan jauzika eta
korrika, elkarri keinuak eginez antzerki batean bezala,
eta hegabera bat, Granadako Fray Luisek zioen moduan,
zauritu itxura egin eta bakar bakarrik zihoan ibai ertzetik
ehiztariak erakarri eta bere kideen etzalekutik desbideratzeko;
multzoka, uxoek hegoranzko lerroari eusten zioten tinko.
Ireki nituen begiak: hegoaizeak hosto bat zeraman herrestan.

Euria eta kazkabarra izan genituen hurrengo joanaldian,
eta ehun bat arkume zeuden ilaran jarrita eta hankatxoak
Zurbaranen "Agnus Dei" laukian bezala loturik zituztela;
Loreei zegokionez, kamelia zen azokako lore bakarra,
baina haren pare zebilen, harro eta apain, kolore moreko aza.
Arrandegietan, milaka antxoen sabelek distira egiten zuten,
eta ugariak ziren, halaber, zuhaitz landareak, hala etxerakoak,
sagar, gerezi, intxaur, gaztaina, piku edo aran emaileak,
nola basokoak, haritzak eta pagoak, pinuak eta urkiak.
Nekazariak esan zuen: "ez dut aldi batean granadarik izango,
baina ilar goxoak nahi badituzue, hementxe dauzkat lehenak."
Begiak itxi eta Mateoren hitzak etorri zitzaizkidan aitaren
ahotsean: begira, arkumeak otso artera lez bidaltzen zaituztet.
Izan zaitezte, ba, sugea bezain zuhurrak, eta uxoa bezain lauak.
Ireki nituen begiak: oinetakoetan kazkabar aleak neuzkan.

Azokara bidean berriro, nartzisoak eta mimosak ikusi genituen
etxe atarietan, eta astotxo bat ere bai saski bete gazta berriekin
oraindik Francis Jammesen mundu xaloan bizi bagina bezalaxe,
eta heldu, eta faiasaiaren arrautzak zeuden salgai txitatzeko,
eta magurdiz egindako mermeladak ontzi handi eta txikietan.
Zenbait posturen paretik pasatzean, berriz, usaina sentitzen zen,
mendarena batzuetan, mihiluarena edo arrosarena bestetan,
eta haiekin nahastuta, arrotz eta harro, baratxuri freskoarena;
Nekazariak esan zuen: "denetik daukat ia, nahi duzuena eskatu,
marrubi, gerezi, San Juan sagar, aran hori, aran gorri, muxika,
baina, tomate, babarrun, tipula, alkatxofa, letxu, erremolatxa;

**THE DAYS GO BY**

We saw walnuts and hazelnuts at the fair, sold by the bag,
and swallows, pigeons and hares the hunters had shot
hanging in a corner, little heads limp on the breast.
There were white mushrooms piled high, and medlars too,
And amongst the flowers, chrysanthemums and lilies reigned.
"I've no tomatoes left, or green beans, hardly a handful of them,"
the farmer told us as she patted her headscarf into place,
likewise with the peppers, they seemed to be the last ones, not many left.
I closed my eyes: in the forest, hares were leaping and
running, gesturing to each other as in a theatre play,
and a swallow, as Fray Luis de Granada used to say,
pretended he'd been hit and fluttered down the river bank, all alone,
to attract the hunters and divert them from where others were hiding;
in groups, pigeons held firmly to the southern line.
I opened my eyes: the southern wind was playing with a leaf.

It rained and hailed next time we went,
there were hundreds of lambs like the one
in Zurbarán's *Agnus Dei*, their little legs tied.
As for flowers, camellias filled the fair,
though purple cabbages, so proud and elegant, captured the eye.
At the fishmonger's stall, the bellies of thousands of anchovies sparkled,
and there were many young trees, ready to be planted in the garden,
apple, cherry, walnut, chestnut, fig or plum;
and forest trees, oaks and beeches, pines and birches.
The farmer said: "There won't be any pomegranates for a while,
but if you'd like some tasty beans, here are the first of the season."
I closed my eyes and heard Matthew's words in my father's
voice: See, I am sending you out like sheep into the midst of wolves;
so be wise as serpents and innocent as doves.
I opened my eyes: there were hailstones on my shoes.

On the way to the fair once again, we saw narcissi and mimosas
in every doorway, and also a little donkey carrying a basketful of cheeses,
almost as if we were still living in the good old days of Francis Jammes;
and when we arrived, there were pheasant eggs for sale, ready to hatch,
and raspberry jam in jars big and small.
As we walked by the stalls we caught the scents,
here of marjoram, there of fennel, then roses;
and around them all, piquant and full, the smell of fresh garlic.
The farmer said: "I've almost everything, ask for whatever you want:
strawberries, cherries, San Juan apples, yellow plums, red plums, peaches,
green beans, tomatoes, onions, broad beans, artichokes, lettuce, beetroot,

ilarrak gutxi, halere, eta onttoak kaxkarrak, eta gereziak berdin."

Itxi nituen begiak: neska-mutil batzuk murgilka zebiltzan ibaian
garrasi batean, ze hotza dagoen ura, ze hotza eta ze ona.
Ireki nituen begiak: nekazariak marrubi bat jarri zidan ahoan.


## BIZITZAK EZ DU ETSITZEN

Bizitzak ez du etsitzen
ezpada muga latzetan;
ezpadu Oihanarekin egiten amets,
egiten du Desertuarekin.

Eta hala, Iraila garo gorridunak,
soilik Elur, soilik Otso,
Barren zabal eta izoztu
izan nahiko zukeen;

Eta izan nahiko zukeen Eguzkiak
Argi huts eta zorrotz
Erleen memoria ahulean;

Gaua, berriz,
hastapenetako garaiaz
oroitzen da bereziki,
orduan ez baitzen Gaua besterik;

Era berean, Sekula ez
edo Beti Beti
esanka dabil nire bihotza;
Bi hitz bakarretan
bere desira guztiak.

a few kidney beans; wild mushrooms are quite scarce this year, so are the cherries."
I closed my eyes: some boys and girls were splashing in the river,
screaming how cold the water is, how cold and how nice.
I opened my eyes: the farmer put a strawberry in my mouth.

## LIFE

Life knows only
thorny extremes.
When not Jungle,
Desert.
It dreams no more.

And so, this September of
Red Ferns
wants only
Snow,
and Wolf;
aims at being bare,
frozen Immensity.

And Sun dreams
of Light pure and sharp,
blinding memory
of Bees.

While Night
remembers fondly
that first moment
of only night.

And so
Never, Never,
or,
Always, Always,
loudly beats my Heart.
Measuring
against those two words, unfortunately,
all desires.

**BIZITZA BIZITZA DA**

Bizitza bizitza da,
eta ez bere emaitzak.

Ez mendi baten gailurrean
eraikitako etxe sendoa,
edo etxe horretako apaletan
kokaturiko koroa eta dominak,
urrezkoak edo urre itxurakoak.
Ez hori bakarrik bizitza.
Bizitza bizitza da.

Ez hiri edo nazio urrunetara
egindako bidaia alaiak,
edo urrun horietan ikusitako
haur, andre eta gizon bitxiak,
ondo edo gaizki fotografiatuak.
Ez hori bakarrik bizitza.
Bizitza bizitza da.

Ez euriaren hotsa sabaian,
edo kazkabarrarena leihoetan,
ez elurra, ez ilargi isila,
ez argia bera ere, zoragarria,
uda berokoa edo negu hotzekoa.
Ez hori bakarrik bizitza.
Bizitza bizitza da.

Ez andre hori edo gizon hura
belarrira xuxurlaka ari zaiguna,
ez gurasoak, ez semealabak,
ez anaiarreba edo lagunak ere,
lehengoak eta betikoak.
Ez hori bakarrik bizitza.
Bizitza bizitza da.

**LIFE IS LIFE**

Life is life,
not its consequences.

Not the solid house
built on a mountain top,
or the gold-plated
trophies and medals
crowding its shelves.
Life isn't just that.
Life is life.

Not the journeys
to faraway cities,
or the children, men
and women photographed
there, badly or beautifully.
Life isn't just that.
Life is life.

Not the rain on the roof,
or hail on the windows,
or the snow, or the quiet moon,
or the light, so wonderful,
yellow in summer and white in winter.
Life isn't just that.
Life is life.

Not the woman or the man
who whispers in our ear,
not our parents, or children,
not our brothers or sisters, or friends,
new or old.
Life isn't just that.
Life is life.

**BI KANTU**

### CANCIÓN TONTA

Me moriré, dubidubí
Me moriré, dubidubá
Es posible, dubidubí
Casi seguro, dubidubá
Pero, ¿quién me matará?

Quizá me mate
El terrible Uno,
O su hermanito,
El pequeño Dos;
Probabilidades
Tienen el Tres
El Cuatro y el Cinco,
Y también el Seis.
Pero en Noviembre
Mi favorito
Es el Siete
De la suerte.

Me moriré, dubidubi
Me moriré, dubidubá
Es probable, dubidubí
Casi seguro, dubidubá
Pero, ¿quién me matará?

El Ocho, tan amarillo
Puede ser él mi asesino,
O el Nueve lluvioso
Si tiene buen tino.
Y habrá una noche
Entre el Diez y el Once
Que de paseo
Quizá me lleve.
Y el mismo Doce,
Aunque es bueno,
Al Trece envidia
De vez en cuando.
Hasta el Catorce
Tan anodino
Aguarda con un cuchillo.

## TWO SONGS

### SILLY SONG

I'll die, doobeedoobee
I'll die, doobeedoobaa
it's possible, doobeedoobee
almost certain, doobeedoobaa
But who'll do me in?

Maybe the scary First
will be my death,
or maybe its little bro',
the tiny Second.
Third and Fourth
and Fifth, and Sixth
are in the running too.
But in November
my favourite number
is the lucky Seventh.

I'll die, doobeedoobee
I'll die, doobeedoobaa
it's possible, doobeedoobee
almost certain, doobeedoobaa
But who'll do me in?

The ever-brighter Eighth,
may be my murderer,
or rainy Ninth,
if it gets here on time.
And maybe one night,
sometime between
the Tenth and the Eleventh,
I'll be taken away.
And the Twelfth itself,
so kind most days,
now and then resents
Thirteenth's bad press.
And even the Fourteenth,
so meek and mild,
waits somewhere with a knife.

Me moriré, dubidubí
Me moriré, dubidubá
Es probable, dubidubí
Casi seguro, dubidubá
Pero, ¿quién me matará?

No quiero morir
El día Quince,
Ni tampoco el Dieciséis,
Y el Diecisiete
A decir verdad
Me viene bastante mal.
Y el Dieciocho lo mismo
Por una cuestión
Sentimental.
El Diecinueve
No sería natural,
El Veinte suena fatal,
Del Veintiuno
Y del Veintidós
Prefiero no hablar.

Me moriré, dubidubí
Me moriré, dubidubá
Es posible, dubidubí
Casi seguro, dubidubá
Pero, ¿quién me matará?

El Veintitrés
Saldré a la calle,
El Veinticuatro
Estaré en Bagdag;
El Veinticinco
Me iré a Ispahan
Tranquilamente;
Encuéntrame si puedes!
El Veintiséis
Y el Veintisiete
Comeré manazanas;
Envenénalas si te atreves!

I'll die, doobeedoobee
I'll die, doobeedoobaa
it's possible, doobeedoobee
almost certain, doobeedoobaa
But who'll do me in?

I don't want to die
on the Fifteenth,
or the Sixteenth,
and to tell you the truth
the Seventeenth
is *très* inconvenient.
And the Eighteenth too,
it won't do,
I'll be in Kathmandu.
On the Nineteenth?
What do you take me for,
a fool?

And on the Twentieth... ugh!
About the Twenty-first
and the Twenty-second,
let's just say... nope.

I'll die, doobeedoobee
I'll die, doobeedoobaa
it's possible, doobeedoobee
almost certain, doobeedoobaa
But who'll do me in?

On the Twenty-third
I'm going out,
on the Twenty-fourth
I'll be in Baghdad;
on the Twenty-fifth
in Isfahan,
and so what,
find me if you can!
On the Twenty-sixth
and Twenty-seventh
I'll be eating apples,
will you poison them?

El Veintiocho
Iré a nadar,
El Veintinueve
Flotaré tan ricamente
Si de los remolinos
Sacar provecho sabes.

Me moriré, dubidubí
Me moriré, dubidubá
Es posible, dubidubí
Casi seguro, dubidubá
Pero, ¿quién me matará?

El Treinta por ser par,
El Treintaiuno porque no lo es,
Los dos son criminales
Profesionales,
Habitan en las salas
Terminales
De los hospitales;
Saben mucho de finales


**EGUN FINLANDIAR BAT**
*Garikanorekin hizketan telefonoz*

Egun finlandiar bat
Egun finlandiar luze bat
Berrogei egun arrunten
Luzerakoa behar dut.

Egun finlandiar bat nahi nuke
Zurekin hiketan jarraitzeko
Aztertzeko nola bizi
Paradisutik kanpora

Finlandiako zerua urdina da
Eta udaran are eta urdinago,
Eguzkiak laranja bat ematen du,
Eta ilargiak berdin, beste laranja bat.

On the Twenty-eighth
I'll go for a swim,
on the Twenty-ninth
I'll float along happily,
so if eddies are your thing
you know what needs doing!

I'll die, doobeedoobee
I'll die, doobeedoobaa
it's possible, doobeedoobee
almost certain, doobeedoobaa
But who'll do me in?

The Thirtieth is even
and the Thirty-first is not,
they are both criminals,
trained professionals,
they haunt
terminal patients
in every hospital.
Their word
is final.

**A FINNISH DAY**
    *to Garikano on the phone*

A Finnish day.
I need a long Finnish day
the length of
forty normal days.

I'd like a Finnish day
to keep talking to you.
To figure out how to live
outside Paradise.

The sky in Finland is blue,
and bluer still in summer.
The sun looks like an orange,
and the moon too, another orange.

Egun finlandiar bat nahi dut,
Egun finlandiar luze bat.
Laster aurkituko dugu, maitea,
Paradisuaz kanpora bizitzeko modua.

I want a Finnish day,
a long Finnish day.
Soon, my love, we'll know
how to live outside Paradise.

# FELIPE  JUARISTI

PHOTO: ZALDI ERO

FELIPE JUARISTI was born in Azkoitia in 1957 and stud-
ied journalism and sociology at the Universidad Complu-
tense in Madrid. He was one of the founding members
of the magazines *Porrot* and *Literatur Kazeta* and has
worked as an editor in the Baroja and Bermingham pub-
lishing houses. At present he is a regular contributor to
several newspapers and magazines. He has been a mem-
ber of the Basque Academy of Letters since 2005.

Felipe Juaristi's literary career has been rich and var-
ied, not only because he has experimented with differ-
ent genres (poetry, narrative and children's and young
people's literature), but also because he has received
many prizes. These include the Lizardi Prize for children's
literature in 1992, the Euskadi Poetry Prize in 1998, the
Euskadi Young People's Literature Prize in 2000, the Leer
es Vivir Prize in 2001, and the 2002 Rosalía de Castro Prize
awarded by the PEN club, Galicia, to honour his entire
literary career. He has also been awarded the Spanish
Critics' Prize several times for his poetry collections.

Juaristi is also a novelist and prolific literary transla-
tor – Maupassant, Wilde, Zimnik, Futrelle, Breytenbach,
Grossman, Celaya, Mirande, Aramburu and Otxoa are
amongst the writers he has translated.

He has taken part in numerous international festivals
and his poems have been included in anthologies and
published in magazines worldwide.

\*\*\*

Berdin da Mendebaldea eta Ekialdea
metafisika eta Poesia nahastea.
Iraganak ez du deus balio
gauza guztiak gastatu
eta adioa eta agurra,
arrats beherako zaldunak,
armadura beltzez janzten direnean. Ezta geroak ere,
sexurik ez baitu.
Gaua naufrago urbanoa da,
ametsak lehorreratzen dira
Elkanorengandik ikasitako ibileraz,
krepuskuloan gerrarik sinestezinenak gertatzen dira,
biziak eta hilak azken tangoa dantzatzen dute
ardo botila baten soinupean,
eternitatearen besarkada izotzezkoa dela,
eta Zientziaren Arbolak sagarrik ez,
itzal hurbila baizik, ematen duela jakin gabe.

## SMOOTHY

Batek badaki hitzak ez direla urrutira joaten
hegoak hautsirik dauzkatelako
aingeru zaurituak bezala.
Hala ere gogoratzen dut
hitzek etxe zaharra betetzen zutenean
gero hiltzeko ikasleen apunteetan
edo memoria nagi baten deserrian.
Eta hitzen atzetik ahots urduri bat
eta ahotsen atzetik defentsarik gabe neu pentsatzen
nola isuriko ote ziren zure hitzak ondoko gelan,
mordoska larrosaren petaloak bezala
edo banan bana sagarrondoaren hostoak bezala.

\*\*\*

It makes no difference, mixing West with East
metaphysics with poetry.
The past is worth little
when everything is worn
and farewell and goodbye,
the horsemen of sundown
wear their black armour.
And the future is just as bad,
sexless thing.
Night is an urban shipwreck
and dreams disembark
at Elcano's leisurely pace.
The most unthinkable wars happen at dusk,
the dead and the living dance the last tango
to the tinkling of bottles of wine.
The forgotten deny
that the embrace of eternity is ice,
and that the Tree of Science harbours only
a partial ability to shade,
branches tangled with mistletoe,
and not a single apple.

## SMOOTHY

It is common knowledge that words never go far
because their wings are broken
like fallen angels'.
However, I remember a time
when words filled an old house
and eventually died in students' notebooks,
or were condemned to exile in their lazy memories.
And behind the words a tremulous voice
and behind the voice, me, defenceless; I think
about how the words fall on the floor in the next room,
clustered like rose petals
or one by one like leaves from an apple tree.

Bazegoen patioan magnolio bat ia eskola-mugan
baina beste mundua sortzen zuen haren gerizak.
Lanagatik nekatuta – esate baterako –
esertzen ginenean ama batek bezala hartzen gintuen.
Aspertuta joanik sosegatzen ginen haren altzoan
eta etxe zaharreko hitzak ez ziren gugana iristen.

Itsasoan Akab kapitainak bale handia bezala
lore zuri bat irekitzen ikusten genuen.
Bakarrik magnolioak erakusten zerbait

## METROPOLIS 2

Hala entzun zuen ametsetan ziotela:
"inork ez du bere burua ezagutzen
Sorterritik joanik ez bada.
Mugimendu hutsa da gizakia"
Iratzartzean bista zuen altxatu.
Dena zegoen geldi eta lasai:
Etxea, kea zeriola tximiniatik,
Atarian, berak aldatutako ezkia loretan.

Alde egin zuen atzean utzirik
Etxea, kea, ataria, ezkia.
Oinen soinua oihartzunak ezin harrapa.
Elurraren oroitza begietan zera –
Maten ibaiak zituen gainditu,
Mendi zuriak hodeiez inguratuak.
Lur lehorrak ikusi zituen, lur hezeak,
Eta eguzki bera zeruetan zaindari.
Ia ukitu zuen behatzekin ortzemuga,
Perlazko haria urruntasunaren lepoan,
Eta ilargi bera, zeruetan zaindari.
Gazte egin zen, gizon beranduago.
Zilar kolorez jantzi zitzaion ilea.

There was a magnolia tree in the playground, by the road,
and its shade projected an alternate world.
When we tired from work – so to speak –
we sat there and felt the embrace of a mother.
If we arrived exasperated its calm would lull us,
voices from the old house couldn't reach that far.

As Captain Ahab contemplated the great whale at sea,
so we watched as a white flower opened.
Only the magnolia tree taught us something.


## METROPOLIS 2

He heard a voice in his dreams:
"You'll never know yourself unless
you leave the land of your birth.
Being is pure motion."
Waking, he looked up.
All was still and quiet:
the house, the chimney smoke,
the birch he planted in the doorway, now in leaf.

He took off, leaving behind
the house, the smoke, the doorway, the birch tree.
The echo couldn't keep up with his footsteps.
He crossed rivers that brought
memories of snow to his eyes,
white mountains shrouded in clouds.
He saw cracked earth and fertile soil,
and saw the sun ruling far above.
His fingers came close to the line of the horizon.
a string of pearls around the neck of infinity,
and he saw the moon ruling far above.
Youth came, manhood soon followed.
Silver threads ran through his hair.

Hala entzun zuen ametsetan ziotela:
"Igotzen dena oro da jaisten.
Joaten dena beti etortzen.
Bizitza da etengabeko itzulia.
Ziba baten gisa jiratzeari utz iezaiozu.
Zeure burua aurkitu nahi baduzu
Bila ezazu zeure baitan!"

Hil ondoren lur eman diote
Mutikotan haren eskuek aldatutako zuhaitz
Pean. Dena zegoen geldi eta lasai.
Etxea, kea zeriola tximiniatik.
Orduan konturatu da goizeko hozkirrian
Hezurrak hantxe egon direla beti
Urte eta urte gehiagoren hautsetan bilduak.
Haizeak adargoiak ditu astintzen.
Memoria du deika:
"Baina zer aurkitu duzu ibilian?
Izpiritua baita bidaiari bakartia"

Beste izpirituak aurretik abandonatua
Ez besterik. Iraganean izanaren arrasto zuria.


**PANAMAKO ISTMOA**

Hitzaren tenploak ez gaitu sostengatu
Ispilu hautsiak, zuhaitz doilorrak
Hainbeste tristura, hainbeste tristura
Panamako istmoa ez da estura
Neskatxa birjinen mirakulu geometrikoa
Euriaren teorema grabedadearen aldekoa
Istmo guztiak haragia gorriak
Nora doaz? Nora goaz?
Hatsak, ametsak, ur-errautsak
Ateak irekirik itsasontzi patagonikoak bidaiari
Sarasateren arrabita, Ravelen boleroa
Capricho Vasco, Guridiren gurdia
Iradierren usoa La Habanatik
Soka herdoilduen pianoa
Iratxoen dantzaldia zinema-ikuskizun

He heard a voice in his dreams:
"All that goes up must come down,
what goes must return.
Life is a *perpetuum mobile*.
Stop spinning.
Look inside
to find yourself."

After he died they buried him
under the tree he had planted as a child.
Everything was still and quiet.
The house, the chimney smoke.
In the morning chill he realised
his bones were always there
mixed in with the dust of the years.
The treetops sway.
Memory speaks:
"So, what did you find as you wandered?
The spirit is a lonely pilgrim."

Only what other spirits left behind.
Vanishing vestiges of what was.


**THE ISTHMUS OF PANAMA**

The temple of words no longer sustains us
broken mirrors, miserable trees
such sadness, such sadness
the isthmus of Panama is not a strait
a young virgin's geometric miracle
rain's theorem against gravity
all the naked isthmuses,
where did they go? where did we go?
sighs, dreams, ashen waters
Patagonian vessels open their doors: inside travel
Sarasate's violin, Ravel's bolero,
Basque caprice, Guridi's farmhouse
Iradier's faithful dove from La Havana
a piano's rusty strings
ghostly dancers in cinemascope

Kabo guardiaren tronpeta latza
Abiada handiko bagoiak odol karriletan
Kanoiak, gurina, eztitan itoak erleak
Ibai arre guztiek zilingatzen beren Nerbioi
Finlandiako trenak heroien atseden
Berlingo printzesak edaten al du izarren arnorik?
Beren baitatik ihes al dagite zaldi egarriek?
Hainbeste galdera, hainbeste galdera
Kirurgi mahaiko zuri aseptiko errimean

### VANITAS VANITATIS

Sendoa dena oro airean da aienatzen.
Isurkorra mendietatik jaisten.
Elementuen kontrako ez ziren nire ontziak.
Iratxoen izpiritua zurbila da baina ez elurrezkoa.
Arimen ehiztariak safari batean 14.
Paretako paper margotu berrian eskegitzeko.
Oso txukun, oso txukun, PIM PAM PUM
Karriketan haurrak beste inor esertzen ez.
Xake-jokalari orok aita du hil JAKE MATE.
Edipo geurea zeruetan zarena JAKE MATE.
Hiltzaile orok jainkotzat du bere burua
Larrosen labirintoan errege1 itoa.
Arantzak ernetu goriak haren bihotzean.
Usoen hegadatik ihesi gizaki landerra.
Ezaguna eta ezezaguna gure baitan borrokan.
Hurretik entzuten klabikordio baten doinua.
Nota bakoitzean Lepanto 1.
Bizantzioko kurloiek ez dakite zein beren sexua.
Luma arinak esker-aihenak zeru-ortzian.
Ezkongaien pentsamendua zuria ez.
Datorren gaua ez da lehena izango...
Nola mihura sagarrondo abarretan,
Halakoxea da jakitunen hitza.
*Vainglory*, banitatea, xaboiaren maiestatea,
Kearen modura atertuko haizean.
Hari gorrizko amaraun leunetan.

the corporal's bass trumpet
high-speed trains on blood tracks
cannons, butter, bees drowned in honey
all grey rivers carry a Nervión
the Finnish train the heroes' repose
does the Princess of Berlin drink the nectar of stars?
do thirsty horses run from themselves?
such questions, such questions
from the grandiose aseptic white
operating theatre


## VANITY OF VANITIES

Solid dispels everything in the air.
Liquid flows down the mountain face.
My vessels couldn't withstand the elements.
Elves' translucent spirits not of ice.
Soul hunters in a Safari 14.
To hang on the newly-printed wallpaper.
Very wow, very wow, WHAM KAH-POW
Only kids sit on the narrow streets.
All chess players kill fathers CHECK MATE.
Our Oedipus who art in heaven CHECK MATE.
All murderers think they are God.
Asphyxiated ruler in a labyrinth of roses.
Incandescent thorns in his heart.
Wretched runaway from a pigeon's flight.
Known and unknown struggle inside.
Clavichord tones in the distance.
Each note Lepanto 1.
Byzantine sparrows ignorant of their sex.
Floating feathers thank you shoots in heaven.
Fiancée's thoughts unwhite.
The coming night won't be the first...
Why mistletoe in the branches of the apple tree.
Such is the word of the wise.
Vainglory, vanity, the majesty of soap.
Like smoke in the vanishing air.
In red-threaded spider webs.

**PERSPEKTIVA NEVSKY**

1 izatea baino gehiago da bakarrik egotea.
2 izatea baino gehiago, gutxienik.
2 baita interesatzen zaigun guztia.
Eta batzuetan bakarrik egoteak esan nahi du
Batean bizi direla multzoak.

Noizbait bakarrik egon denak
Bereaz gain bizi ditu beste bizitzak,
Aspaldiko oihartzunek hartua diote ezaguera,
Urrutiko musikak ezkutatzen dira haren bihotzean,
Arima lausotzen diote milaka
Jainko ezezagun eta harrizkoren otoitzek.

Noizbait bakarrik egon denak
Bereaz gain ibili ditu beste bideak;
Atsedena bilatu du ilunabar izoztuetan,
Ahantziaren iturria goizalba loretsuetan,
Seguruak, argizko uztaien artean ernalduak.
Badaki zeruertzaren lerroa nahastu egiten dela
Gorputz behin eta berriro maitatu izanarekin.
Ez dagoela beste lurrik atzean geratu dena baino.

Noizbait bakarrik egon dena
Galdu izan da denboraren azpilduretan,
Denbora orainaren oroitzapen luze urezkoan,
Geure baitan dagoena bildurik eta lo
Hondar aleak esku-kuskuilu batean bezala.

Zeren bakarrik dagoena ez baita inondar.
Geografia zaio itsaso ordokiz betea.
Ihesi doa ziurtasunetik, desertore gisa.
Icaro berritua, airean barrena biluzik hegan.
Baina babestuko lukeen tenplurik aurkitzen ez.
Pentsamenduak gorritzen diren lorebaratzerik ez.
Fedearen begiez ez baitu so egiten.

Jakituna izanik inoiz ez da sentitu arrotz.
Joan-etorri dabil, inora mugitu gabe.
Hitz egiten du hitzik gabe, baina esanez
Den guztia badela eta izango dela
Norberak barruan daramanean.

**NEVSKY PROSPECT**

To be alone means to be more than one,
or at least, more than two,
the most interesting number here is two.
Sometimes to be alone means
multitudes live in one.

To have been alone,
to have lived lives other than your own.
Old echoes hit home.
Distant music chides the heart.
The prayers of unknown gods of stone
reverberate.

To have been alone,
to have walked paths other than your own;
requested repose from frozen dusks
the flower of forgetfulness from dawns in bloom,
safe amidst newborn curves of light.
To know the line of the horizon meets
the often-loved body of the beloved,
and the only land is land left behind.

To have been alone,
to have been lost in the folds of time
where long remembrances of the present
sleep curled up,
like grains of sand in a seashell-hand.

Because the loner is a nowherer.
Geography is infinite sea.
Run away from certainty, deserter.
Icarus renewed, airborne, naked.
Can't find a temple for shelter,
a flower garden for thoughts to thrive.
Eyes of faith shut.

Wisdom not to be the stranger,
come and go in stillness.
Speak wordlessly but say
everything that is exists, will exist
once it is within.

Bakarrik dagoenarentzako oroitarririk ederrena
Parke abandonatutako banku hutsa.
Umez eta txori erraustuz inguraturik.

## AUSCHWITZ

Atertu du euria.
Haizea jabaldu da.
Lurra arnasa hartzen hasi.
Ikara dira akaziak,
Besoak zeruari kolpeka.
Txirritak kantatzen
Sagar-hostoak babes.
Hilerrira jotzen duen
Leihoa irekitzen dut.
Erre-usaina dator handik,
Hezur eta ile kiskaliek
Busti egin dute giroa.
Auschwitz datorkit oroimenera,
Euriaren ondorengo
Edozein egunetan.

## BARATZAIN

Odol truk eraiki du mundua, baratzeko baranoan.
Bihotz-arimen atsedenleku, hezur-giharren neurriko.
Mahats-aihenak estali duen horma handiaren kanpoan
Laino artetik ihesi luzatzen dena zaio atzerriko.

Loreak arin ximeltzen dira kolore batean errerik,
Txori inozoek soinu bakarra kantatzen dute airean,
Ez du itsasoa inoiz ezagutu, izokinek ekarririk
Ez bada, ondoko errekatik gora tantaz tanta joatean.

The best homage to the loner
a desolate park, an empty bench,
surrounded by burnt children and birds.

## AUSCHWITZ

No more rain.
The wind becalms.
Earth begins to breathe.
Acacias are afraid,
beat heaven with their fists.
A cicada's song
deep in the foliage of an apple tree.
I open the window,
it overlooks the cemetery.
A burnt smell.
Charred bone and hair
have impregnated the air.
I remember Auschwitz.
Any day
after rain.

## GARDENER

With blood he has raised a world in this garden.
His heart and soul's repose, of flesh and bone dimensions.
The world beyond the great vine-covered wall
far removed amidst the clouds in exile.

Flowers whither quickly, burnt forever into a shade,
silly birds chirrup songs over and over again.
The mystery of the sea brought home by salmon
lapping salty droplets up river.

Buruz daki zuhaitz bakoitzaren izen eta dirdiraldi,
Aski du itzal iluna ikustea zein zer den ziurtatzeko.
Berea ez da hego zorrozturik kalte latz dagien Aldi.
Ez du ezer behar bizitzari men egin eta makurtzeko.

Batzuetan ziztada sakona bat-batean du sumatzen,
Barne-muinak iraultzen dizkio, eta argira atera.
Gosea ezik, maitemina da, oso aspaldiko oroitzapen.
Krabelinek usaina bezala laster galdu zuen hura.

Begiak hertsirik neskatoa dator biluzik gogora,
Gaztain kolore ditu begiak, marrubizkoak ezpainak;
Baratxuriak lakoxe hortzak, adatsa intxaur erara,
Sagar gorri beroak bularrak, laranjazkoak masailak.

Hatzak baratx mugitzen zaizkio, igali ederron bila,
Saski batean gordetzen ditu, albahaka-hostotan bilduak,
Gogobetetzen duen gorputzaren haragi-zati bailira.
Usain sarkorrak bazterrik bazter daramatza grina antzuak.

Mahaian eserita poliki, otoitzean bezala ahoa
Zabal, fruitu bizien irensle, berehala da asea.
Gorputza etzaten du ohe gainean, jabal eta naroa:
Maitasun-frogarik gozoena da maite dena jatea.


## GEOGRAFIA

Bertan jaio naizen arren,
Ez dut ezagutzen nire herria.
Nire hizkuntza bera duen arren,
Ez dut ulertzen nire herria.
Horixe da nire aberria,
Poliki-poliki hiltzen nauena,
Beti itzultzen naizen atzerria,
Gaixo bat bere minera bezala.

He knows the names of trees, their refulgent days,
their dark shadows mark which is which.
His time does not punish with sharpened wings.
With bended knee he succumbs to life.

Sometimes he buckles under a pernicious grip
that hooks his entrails, drags them into light.
It isn't hunger but the pain of a love long lost,
evanescing swiftly, like carnation scent.

Then his eyes close and she comes, naked,
her hazelnut eyes, her strawberry lips,
her chestnut hair, cloves of garlic her teeth,
two warm apples her breasts, with blushing cheeks.

With tenderness his fingers caress the precious fruits
and place them in a wicker basket with basil leaves,
as if they were flesh from the woman in his soul.
His pungent sterile passion fills the air.

He sits still at the table, his lips in prayer,
open, devourer of live fruits, at once satiated.
His body sprawls on the bed, full, content,
it is proof of love to eat your beloved.


**GEOGRAPHY**

I was born here,
yet I don't know this place.
We speak the same language,
yet I don't understand my people.
This is my homeland,
bit by bit she kills me,
yet I always return to her strange domain,
like a sick man to his pain.

\*\*\*

Rembrandtek infinitua nahi du pintatu,
infinitua ekarri nahi du begietara,
hatzetara, belarrietara, haizeetara.
Sendoa, biguna, sakona da
infinitua.
Leihotik begiratzen du,
emakume bat igarotzen da dotore
gazte oraindik,
ura, sua,
Rembrandtek elurra dela uste du.
Ez da usorik zeruan, hodeiek estaltzen dute hiria.
Zuria, iheskorra da zoriona.
Gizon adinean sartuxea igarotzen da,
gurdi batek darama nekea garraio.
*Denbora Denbora Denbora.*
Rembrandtek gaua dela uste du,
euri beltza, itsaso beltza, hiriaren aurrealde beltza,
*Herio, Herio, Herio.*
Soldadu-talde bat igarotzen da,
eguneroko erronda alai zaratatsua,
baso bat kolore guztiak zabal,
txoriak beren lumak harro erakusten.
Begiratu die kristalen atzetik,
baina joanak dira jadanik isilik
zaldun poloniarra, oinezko espainiarra.
Arinak, krudelak dira soldaduen begiak,
gogorrak, distirarik gabeak.
*Azkar Azkar Azkar.*
Infinituaren atzetik beti.

Rembrandtek ezin leihorik itxi,
bizitza igarotzen zaio aurretik,
neska-mutilak jolasean,
herejeak kai berrira kateaz loturik,
erbestea dute helmuga.
Emakume dirudunak mintzo,
Jainkoa dute maite,
Burgesak Burtsa-Etxerantz
ekialdeko geografia dute maite.
*Spinoza Spinoza Spinoza.*

***

Rembrandt wants to paint infinity,
to bring infinity to the eyes
the fingers   the ears   the air
Infinity
dense   soft deep
looks out of the window
an elegant woman passes by
still young   water   fire
Rembrandt thinks she is snow
no pigeons in the sky   clouds cloak the city
happiness   white and elusive
a middle-aged man walks by
a cart   carts   weariness
*Time   Time   Time*
Rembrandt thinks the night is
black rain   black sea   black city façade
*Death   Death   Death*
a regiment passes by
daily patrol   lively   raucous
forest of unfurled colours
proud birds parading their plumage
he watches behind the glass
but they have left in silence
the Polish rider   the Spanish infantryman both lithe
the soldier's eyes are cruel
harsh   lacklustre
*quick   quick   quick*
seeking infinity always

Rembrandt can't close the windows
life passes by
kids play
chained heretics tramp to the quay
towards exile
moneyed women prattle   love God
the bourgeois advance   lovers of Eastern geography
*Spinoza   Spinoza   Spinoza*

Sentimenduen geometra, irritsen esteta
infinitua neurtzen, pauso zalantzazkoez.
Pintatu nahi du, eduki nahi du
ekarri nahi du infinitua argitara;
baina bere pintatzaile irudia besterik ez da ageri.

Infinituaren aurpegiak
txiki ditu begiak.

geometer of feelings   aesthete of passions
measures infinity   with uncertain step
wants to paint it   wants to hold it
wants to bring infinity to the light
but only his own painterly figure emerges

infinity's face
small-eyed.

JOSEBA   SARRIONANDIA

JOSEBA SARRIONANDIA was born in Iurreta in 1958 and holds a degree in Basque philology. He has written for newspapers and literary magazines and translated literary works, and is currently a member of the Basque academy of letters. He was one of the founding members of the literary group POTT, which had a powerful influence in the development of Basque literature in the 1980s. His collaboration with ETA brought about his imprisonment in 1980; he escaped in 1985 and his whereabouts have been unknown since.

He has been quite experimental throughout his literary career and, as well as exploring the traditional genres (poetry, narrative, essay), he has written hybrid texts that explore an innovative concept of literature. He is a renowned short story writer and, more recently, has written novels such as *Lagun izoztua* (The Frozen Friend, 2001) and *Kolosala izango da* (It Will Be Colossal, 2003).

His work as a literary translator has influenced his development as a writer. Some of his translations include T. S. Eliot's 'The Wasteland', Coleridge's 'The Rhyme of the Ancient Mariner' and Fernando Pessoa's *The Mariner*.

It is, however, his career as a poet which has earned him his reputation in the world of contemporary Basque letters, and his first book, *Izuen gordelekuetan barrena* (In the Recesses of Fear, 1984), is an inspiration to many young Basque poets.

**BITAKORA KAIERA**

Ingurubilean barrena abiatu da bidaztia
    noiz eta non sartu den oroitzen ez duen arren.
Bidea ingurubila bat dela suposatzen du, gauza berrietan
    iragandakoen isladak somatzen dituelakotz.
Baina iraganaren isladak ez dira atseginak, izugarriak dira
    zentrorantz amiltzen dela erakusten deraukotelakotz.
    Baina ba dea zentrorik?
    Ala zabalalderantz amiltzen ote da?
Orduan pentsatzen du gordelekua behar duela eta zokoetan
    gordetzen du aldizka bere burua. Baina izuak ere
    bergordelekuetan ezkutatzen dira.
Orduan pentsatzen du noraezean galduko dela eta hari bat
    behar duela labyrinthoan. Baina zer lokarritan
    eutsi haria?
Orduan pentsatzen du oroitzapena bederen sostengatu behar duela
    eta bitakora kaier bat eskribatzen du, ilunabarrero.
Hauxe da noraezaren bitakora kaiera, bidaztiak
    haizerik gabeko itsasoan galerako ekaitza geroago eta
    gertuago somatzen duen lemazainaren antzera idazten du.
Etsipenez eskribatzen du:
    ez prophetaren antzera, eroaren antzera baizik;
    ez Jainkoentzat, marionetentzat baizik;
    marionetak marionetentzat bezala eskribatzen du.
Eta bidaztiak badaki batzutan, baina bertzetan ez daki deusere:
    nor den, bere burua nortzu diren ere.
Batzutan pentsatzen du Europan barrena dabilela
    eulia emakume bilutsiaren gorputzean bezala.
Bertzetan bitakora kaiereko orrialde hutsei begira geratzen da,
    deus ere pentsatu gabe, edo ingurubilak marrazten.

**HIL EGIN DA ORGANISTA**

Smetanaren doinu batek kulunkatzen zuen lehen
Moldavaren urgaina Pragako ziudadelaren ondoan.
Orain, harriak bakardadean, bakardadea harrietan ere
eta bizitza astiro doa, heriotza bezain ezezaguna.
Hemendik gauza ugari ikusten ditu leiho batek:
bizimoduak makalduriko hitzak, keinu etsituak,
oroitzapen erotiko batzu, ihes, irri soil bat.
Leiho batek ikusten du hemendik:

**NAUTICAL LOGBOOK**

The traveller is deep in the spiral
        though he can't remember when or where he entered.
He assumes the road is a spiral, because he detects
        vestiges of the past in things.
But the vestiges of the past aren't nice, they're terrifying,
        they indicate he is plunging towards the core.
        But is there a core?
        Or is he plunging outwards?
And so it occurs to him he needs a hiding place and crawls
into little nooks here and there. But
fear creeps in with him.
And so it occurs to him he is directionless and will get lost, and
        he could do with a thread in this labyrinth. But what
        will he tie the thread to?
And so it occurs to him he must at least secure his memories,
        so he fills in his nautical logbook, nightly, come dusk.
This is the nautical logbook of aimlessness, the traveller
        writes, like a helmsman who foresees
        the storm on the windless sea.
He writes about despair:
        not like a prophet, but like a madman;
        not for the gods, but for the marionettes;
        he writes the way marionettes write for each other.
And sometimes the traveller knows, other times he hasn't a clue
        who he is, who all the people inside him are.
Sometimes he thinks he is trawling through Europe
        the way a fly draws circles around a naked woman's body.
Other times he looks at the blank pages of his nautical logbook
        and thinks nothing, and doodles a spiral.

**THE ORGANIST IS DEAD**

The waters of the river Vltava, near the castle
in Prague, oscillated to one of Smetana's tunes.
Now, the stones are alone, loneliness permeates
them, and life goes on slowly, unpredictable as death.
A window can witness many things from here:
words life has worn away, gestures of resignation,
a few fleeting erotic memories, a single smile.
From here, a window witnesses the following:

Rainer M. Rilke sosaren truke Orfeori poemak eskatzen,
Golem iargi hotzen bila zubietan barrena, eta
Pragako ikasleak izpilu hautsi bat – haunitz – eskuetan.
Hemendik leiho batek ikusten du:
Franz Werfel eta Vladimir Holan egunkaria erostera datozela
goizaldero, beren eskela galduak ea ageri direnentz begira.
eta arlekin noragabeak eltxo hordituak hiltzen,
eta zuhaitzen beldurrez hirira herbesteratu diren guziak
farolen azpian dardaraka. Leiho batek ikusten du:
odol anpuluka negarrez amonak, loak hartzen haien iloba enanoak,
Franz Kafka hausterrak kontatzen.
Leiho batek, halaber, ikusten du organista bat hilik
paper lohi batzu eskuan: "Anton Dvorak-Mundu Berriaren Sinfonia".
Hilik da, inork estaltzen ez duen arren,
eta isilik oro leihoaren begiradan.
Izotzezkoa Moldavaren urgaina,
hotsik gabe doa denbora. Azpitik doa ura.


### ETXERA ITZULI

altxorren mapak besapean
etxea utzi eta ondinen
abestien xerka abiatu ninduzun
izuen gordelekuetan barrena

sukarri urdinarre tipiak
eta oihan beltzetako xokotan
usteltzen diren xoxo habiak soilik
nizkizun bidaian eriden

denborak bidea ahorturik
etxera itzuli ninduzunean
berria zizun ateko zura
eta sarraila ere

Rilke asking Orpheus for poems in exchange for coins,
seeking shrivelled, shivering Golems under bridges, and
Prague students – multitudes – each carrying a broken mirror.
A window witnesses the following from here:
every dawn, as they buy the papers, Franz Werfel and Vladimír Holan
check to see if their missing obituaries have appeared.
And wandering harlequins kill drunken mosquitoes,
and the city migrants, afraid of trees,
tremble under the street lights. The window witnesses:
a grandmother crying floods of blood, her sleeping midget grandchildren,
Franz Kafka counting ashes.
And indeed, a window witnesses a dead organist
clutching a bundle of dirty papers: "Antonín Dvořák – New World Symphony."
He is dead, even though no one has covered him,
and everything is silent under the eyes of the window.
Ice coats the surface of the Vltava,
time passes without sound. Water flows underneath.

### RETURN HOME

laden with treasure maps
you sent me from home
into the recesses of fear
in search of the nymphs' song

all I got for you on my journey
were small grey flint stones
and the rotting nests of blackbirds
that inhabit the belly of dark jungles

time ate up the road
and I returned home to you
and your wooden door was new
and so was your lock

**TREN LUZE BAT**

Beti dago egunsentian tren luze bat
Estaziotik abiatzen.
Andere batek begiratzen du leihotik,
Inori ere ezin dio adio esan.
Beti dago bihotz zatitu bat
Erdiz trenean doana
Eta erdiz estazioan geratzen dena.
Euria erortzen da, kristala bustiaz,
Bagoiak bustiaz, trenbideak bustiaz.
Trena beti infernurantza doa.


**ZAPATA HAUTSI PILA BAT**

Bizitzaren metafora bidaia izan liteke
Heriotza zapata hautsi pila bat da, bere burua
Besterik argitzen ez duen hilargiaren azpian.
Zapata zolek dagoeneko ez dute oroitzen
Beren hamaika pausuetan zer zapaldu duten.
Zapata hautsi pila bat, kordoirik gabe,
Zeren eta kordoiak bidaztiek eraman dituzte
       Beren buruak nonbait urkatzeko.


**PRESO EGON DENAREN GOGOA**

Preso egon denaren gogoa
gartzelara itzultzen da beti.
Kalean juje, fiskal eta
abokatuekin gurutzatzen da
eta poliziek, identifikatu ez arren,
beste inori baino luzeago
begiratzen diote, bere pausua
sosegatua ez delako
edo sosegatuegia delako.
Bihotz barruan
betirako kondenatu bat darama.

## A LONG TRAIN

Sunrise, and always a long train
leaving the station.
A woman looks out of the window,
says goodbye to no one.
And always a heart torn in two:
one half goes on the train,
the other stays on the platform.
Rain falls, wetting the windows,
wetting the wagons, wetting the train tracks.
Always the train is hell-bound.

## A PILE OF BROKEN SHOES

The journey could be a metaphor for life.
Death a pile of broken shoes under the moonlight
that shines solely for its own benefit.
After a lifetime of steps the soles
no longer remember what they've walked on.
A pile of broken shoes bereft of shoelaces,
because the travellers have taken them all
        to go and hang themselves somewhere.

## THE EX-PRISONER'S MIND

The ex-prisoner's mind
always returns to jail.
He sees judges, public prosecutors
and lawyers on the streets, everywhere,
and, even if they fail to identify him,
policemen stare at him
longer than anyone else, because
his walk looks unrelaxed
or maybe too relaxed.
In his heart
he forever carries a condemned man.

### LITERATURA ETA IRAULTZA

Angel Martinez komisarioak bere errebolberraren
    kainoia detenitu biluziaren uzkira sartu
Eta mirila zikindua, odoldua, patetikoa ateratzean
    zer axola zaio mutil torturatuari
        poeta *um fingidor* den ala ez?
G.K. Chesterton-ek bisitatu du La Salve?
Intxaurrondoko kalabozoetan nork ezagutzen du
        Hermann Broch?
Zelan esplikatuko du gero mutil torturatuak
    epailearen aurrera suntsiturik iristean
        *objetive correlative* espresioaren esanahia?
Zer da Molly Bloom-entzat Carabanchelgo
    egunsenti jostorratzez betea?
Nor da Michel Foucault zigor zeldetan
    hamar hilabetez higatzen denarentzat?
        Bost minutuko bisita bat? Enkontru liriko bat?
Presoek Jean Duvoisin-en Biblia estudiatu behar dute
    beren gutun debekatuetan h-ak eta komak
    leku egokian jartzeko?
Zein da literaturarentzat errebeldiaren, iraultzaren,
    mentura ororen balio etiko ahortezina?
Zer izkiriatu da *Voprosi Literaturi* edo *Tel Quel* aldizkarien
    ertzean euskal presoen gose greba amaigabeetaz?
Zer axola zaio *konpromezua* polizien tiro artean
    – bere bihotza erreboluzioaren bandera legez
    ezkutarik gabe – ihes doan mutilari?

### IHESLARIAREN EKIPAIA

Balizko paradisutik egotziak, benetako
    infernutik itzuriak,
aldean daramagu erregunea. Nagusiek gu bizirik
    ala hilda
harrapatzeko aginduak zabaltzen dituzten artean,
    lagunek aterpea ematen digute.
Sorterriko albisteak igurikatzen ditugu,
    irratiak ez du berririk eman;
iada aspaldian, udan, aittitte hil zen,
    ez jakin amama biziko den oraindik.
Hainbeste aduanatako goardiek errekisaturiko

**LITERATURE AND REVOLUTION**

When superintendent Ángel Martínez shoves the barrel
        of his revolver into the anus of the naked prisoner
and the sight comes out dirty, bloodied, pathetic-looking,
        what does it matter to the tortured boy
                if the poet is *a pretender*, as Pessoa said?
Did G. K. Chesterton ever visit La Salve?
Is there anyone in the cells of Intxaurrondo who knows
                Hermann Broch?
When he faces the judge, utterly destroyed,
        how can the tortured boy explain
                the meaning of the *objective correlative*?
How would Molly Bloom understand a sunrise
        of knitting needles in Carabanchel prison?
Who is Michel Foucault to the man who's spent ten months
        withering in a cell?
                A five-minute visit? A lyrical encounter?
Do prisoners study Jean Duvoisin's Basque Bible
        to make sure the commas and aitches in their forbidden letters
                are correct?
Is there an inherent ethical value in rebellion,
        revolution, courage, for literature? No one says.
Has anything been written in literary journals like *Voprosi Literaturi*
        or *Tel Quel* about the Basque prisoners on perennial hunger strikes?
How can he care about *compromise*, the boy on the run, dodging
        police bullets, his naked heart a revolutionary flag?

**A RUNAWAY'S LUGGAGE**

Banished from hypothetical paradise,
                escapees of real Hades,
leaden with guilt. Far and wide
                the chiefs
order us captured dead or alive,
                our friends shelter us.
We await news from the motherland,
                the radio has nothing to offer;
Grandfather died a long time ago, in summer,
                maybe Grandmother is still alive.
Under the bed the suitcase

maleta ohepean utzita
leiho parean eseri eta soegiten dugu kanpora:
elurra jauzkera.
Beste gramatika bat ikasi dugu, halaera hatzamarraz
seinalatzen gaituzte: "Hori arrotza da".
Ez gara egundo itzuliko apika, itzuliko ginela
zirudien lekura,
itzuli nahi genukeen lekura, gure sorlekua
ez ezik, geu ere aldatuko garelako.
Ez zaigu ba ezpain mututako mintzaira hau
elur birrin hori bezala jauziala urtzen...
Leihotik behatzen dugu kanpoa, elurbustia
estartak estaltzen.
Etxeak, ihes egin behar balitz, baditu ate bat
eta hiru leiho.


### MINOTAUROARENAK

Knok knok knok jo dit atea Minotauroak.
"Garagardorik?" galdetu dit
bere ohizko bisitaren atxakia lez, eta
hozkailuruntz noala
entzun dut: "Ezin diagu erretolika egiten
jarraitu."
Garagardo hotz bana mahai gainera atera
Eta eseri garenean esan dit:
"Inork esan ez deuan gauza bat esanen deuat"
eta
idi begiz begiratu nau "Ez diagu aberririk
aldean daramagunaz besterik,
bizitzeko nahi genuen aberria sortzeko
ahaleginean galdu diagu,
eta harrezkero ez diagu ez genuena
ez nahi genuena".
Minotauroa bere apatxei begira gelditu da
une batez:
"Harrezkero, itzuliez gero ere ez gaituk
ginenera itzuliko,
eta ez diagu nahi genuena ezagutuko,
herbestean ibiliko gaituk beti,

many customs' inspectors have searched.
We sit by the window and look at the world outside:
        watch the snow fall.
We have learnt new grammar rules, but fingers still point:
        "He is not from here."
And now we won't return to the place
        we thought we would return to,
the place we hoped to return to, the motherland,
        because, among other things, we are no longer ourselves.
Well, this language of muted lips shall not melt
        as it falls, like that snowflake.
From the window we watch the world outside,
        the sleet falling on footpaths.
If escape becomes necessary, the house has one door
        and three windows.


**THE MINOTAUR SPEAKS**

The Minotaur knock, knock, knocks on my door.
        "Any beer?" he asks,
which is his usual reason for a visit, and
        as I go to the fridge
I hear him say: "We can't keep practising
        rhetoric."
I put two cold beers on the table
        and, sitting down, mumble:
"You're saying what no one else will say",
        and turning
his bovine eyes to me, he responds: "We have no
        motherland but the one inside;
the motherland we hoped to create
        we lost in the attempt,
and since then we don't have the one we had,
        the one we didn't want."
The Minotaur stares at his hooves for a while
        and says:
"Now, even if we return we'll never be
        as we were,
nor will we ever have what we wanted,
        we'll wander aimlessly

sustrairik gabe, haizea bezala." Beste
   garagardo bana atera dudalarik
Minotauroak jarraitu du: "Ez gaituk bertakoak
      inon izanen,
ez hangoak, ez hemengoak, gure eginak alferrik
     galduko dituk nahinon,
izan geure baitakoak ere ez gaituk izanen,
  mila harik honuntz harunzka bultzatuak,
ilusioarekin eta ilusiorik gabe, halabeharrez
   egiten dugun ibilean."
Zutitu eta, aldegin orduko, erantsi du:
  "Herbestean biziko gaituk edonon."

(Grekera zaharrez mintzatu zait eta nik, grekeraz
  batere ez dakidanez gero, ondo ulertu diot.)


## PROPOSAMEN POETIKOA

Halabeharra krudela izan zen gurekin
   poeta bihurtu ginduenean.
Poesia ez da futuroz kargaturiko harma bat,
   beste Gabriel harek nahi zukeenez.
Futuroa gainera – izan gaitezen serioak –
   polbora bustia da.

Ez dut gure fatu tristea zaildu nahi,
   ofizio lagunok,
baina, hitz eder eta ez hain eder
   ugari izkiriatu dugu,
ia denok egin dugu letraren bat
   kantari famaturen batentzat,

denoi itzuli digute testuren bat
   antologiaren baterako.
ia denok idatzi dugu enkarguz
   bideo gidoi bat,
ia denoi eman digute sariren bat
   lausengu eta guzi,

in exile, rootless, like the wind." I take out
        two more beers and
the Minotaur goes on: "We'll never belong
                  anywhere,
we won't be from here or there; whatever we do
               will be lost in the ether, and
the truth is, all along, we weren't honest with ourselves,
       we followed random, uncertain threads,
both with and without hope; we made up our destinies
         as we went along."
He stands up and before leaving adds:
      "We will live in exile, wherever that is."

(He addresses me in ancient Greek throughout, and though
       I don't know a word of it, I understand everything.)


**POETIC PROPOSAL**

Destiny was most cruel
        when it made us poets.
Poetry isn't a weapon loaded with future,
        like that Gabriel guy proposed.
Besides, the future – c'mon, seriously –
        is wet gunpowder.

I don't mean to complicate our sad fate,
        my fellow lyricists,
but we have written enough brilliant and
        mediocre verse,
almost all of us have penned words
        for a famous singer's songs,

all of us have had a thing or two translated
        for an anthology,
almost all of us have produced a script
        on commission,
we have all received an award or two
        and enjoyed the flattery,

denok dugu gure latifundioa edo
        minifundioa egunkarietan,
oroimin belak hazi eta mintzaira kaskabelak
        jo ditugu eta, orain,
lore jokoen ondoren, zer iruditzen zaizue
        poesia egiten hasten bagara?

we are all of us big- or small-time players
    in the mud field that is journalism,
we have all unfurled the sails of memory, tinkled
    the bells of virtuosity, and now,
after all the poetry slams etc., what do you say
    we actually start writing poems?

# RIKARDO ARREGI

PHOTO: ZALDI ERO

Rikardo Arregi Diaz de Heredia was born in Gasteiz in 1958. He studied psychology and trained as a teacher at Salamanca University, and studied Basque philology at the University of the Basque Country. He currently works as a secondary school teacher.

He published his first collection of poetry, *Hari Hauskorrak* (Fragile Threads), in 1993, and received the Spanish Critics' Prize for it. In 1998 he wrote *Kartografia* (Cartography), which was also awarded the Spanish Critics' Prize. Arregi's poems have been included in recent Basque poetry anthologies as well as various anthologies published in Spanish, German, Slovenian, Brazilian Portuguese and Galician. He has also been widely published in magazines.

Arregi is a regular contributor to the Basque press for which he often writes leading articles and reviews, and he has taken part in many literary festivals. He has participated with other writers in collaborative translations of poetry by the Polish Nobel laureate Wisława Szymborska, and Portuguese poets such as Sophia de Melo, Eugénio de Andrade and Jorge de Sena. He has also translated the work of the Spanish poet Ernestina de Champourcin into Basque. Other recent translations by Arregi include the works of contemporary poets Brane Mozetič, Jacek Dehnel, Cathal Ó Searcaigh and Kārlis Vērdiņš.

### KALEAN ERORI PAPERAK

Eta asfalto bustian ziren islatzen
kaleko argi desberdinak, iraunkorrak.
Lipar batez bizi eta hil eta bizi
planeta bakar baten begi ilunetan.
Haizeak puzten ditu izara hezeak
irudi abstraktuak osatuz temati.
Eta gu bestaldean babesaren bila,
eulia bezala negua iristean,
eulia elur gorritan harrapaturik.
Eta nori esan, edo nola, edo noiz,
segundo batean ispiluak dakarren
alkimia: eskalerik eskaleena.
Egunero ordu beretsuan kalea
zeharkatzen zuen huraxe, adibidez.
Gogoan ditugu egun eta etxeak,
egia atsegin genuen garai haiek.

Busti ziren kalean erori paperak
eta tinta nabarra zerien hitzei.
Etorkizunetik datozkigu engoitik
oroitzapenak.

### LUR LOKARTUA III

Ordokietan zehar nekaezin
hemen gutxi mintzatzen da helmugaz,
bideaz egiten da solasa, eta basoez.
Helmugak errauts dezake agian
bidaian bilduriko ezagutza eta begiradak.
Eta lotan zaude ene haragiak
esnaturik nahi zaituenean.
Orduan bakarrik izan daitezke kontsolabide
laino eta literaturaz egindako tren mitikoak.
Itzalen artetik ametsak gauzatzen,
eta amesgaiztoak.
Soldaduak etxerako bidean alai.
Familia bisitatzera doan emakumea,
urtean behin, badakizue.
Itxura garrantzi gutxikoa da hemen

## PAPERS ON THE PAVEMENT

And they burn into the wet asphalt,
the reflections of the many street lights.
Blinkingly they live and die and live
in the dark glistening orb of a solitary planet.
Fearless, the wind inflates the damp sheets
sketching shapes.
And we on the other side search shelter
like flies in winter,
flies entrapped in the bitter snow.
And who will hear this, and when, and how
to explain this sudden alchemy of mirror:
this monstrous beggar?
Maybe that very same person
who crosses the street every day
at the same time, that's who.
We remember days and houses,
an era when we were fond of truth.

They got wet, my papers that fell on the pavement,
turbid ink flew from the words,
and as from now,
memories here from the future.

## THE SLEEPING LAND III

On our tireless journey across these flatlands
destination isn't something we talk about much,
our conversations concern the road, the forests.
Maybe because destination is something that could turn to ashes
the familiarity and the understanding we've gained in this time.
And you sleep when my flesh
wants you awake.
Only the mythical trains built of
clouds and literature console me then.
Dreams emerge from the shadows,
and nightmares.
A soldier, happy on his way home.
A woman, visiting her family
once a year – you know the story.
Appearances are not a matter of concern here

eta denbora geltokietan neurtzen da soilik.
Trubetzkoi eta iraultzaile erromantikoak,
abendua gehiegi maite zuten haiek.
Xake jokalariak. Haur lasaiak.
Neba-arreba gazteak, ederrenak.
Eta Puxkin agertu ahala esnatu egiten zen gizona:

*Ez, bizitzak ez nau gogaitzen.*
*Bizitza maite dut, bizi nahi dut,*
*gaztaroa ihesean ikusi arren*
*ez zait gogoa hozten.*
*Ene jakinminari pozgarri zaizkio oraindik*
*fantasiaren amets maiteak,*
*sentsazio oro.*

Arin doa Puxkinen hegatsa
ibai maiteminduen gainetik.
Hau ez da literatura, zeren lur lokartuan
ibaiak ere maitemintzen baitira, adibiderik bada.
Eta gero Tatiana Nikolaievna. Lauaxetaren
marinel eta txo mozkortuak, ederrenak.

Hilobien aurreko mahai eta eserleku
zurezkoak, itzalekin hitz egin eta bazkaltzeko.
Izen bat eta bi data.
Usolie-Sibirskoie bigarren dataren ondoan
idatziko balute, bai dotorea ene hilarria.
Eta Puxkin agertu ahala esnatu egiten zen gizona:

*Zer esan nahi du zuretzat nire izena?*
*Oroigarri bakarra*
*paper batean utziriko aztarna hila*
*hilartitzaren antzera,*
*letra arraroz idatzita*
*inork ulertzen ez duen hizkuntza batean.*

Eta gero haurrak ur ertzean jolasean.
Iragana eta iraganaren oroimena
saltzera beharturik zegoen emakumea.
Listvianka-ko elizaren aurrean belarritakoez,
bereaz eta nireaz, eta haien esanahiez
mintzatu zitzaidan mutil urduria, ederrena.
Eta Puxkin agertu ahal esnatu egiten zen gizona:

and time is only measured in terms of stops and stations.
Trubetzkoy and the Romantic revolutionaries,
the ones who loved December too much.
Chess players. Quiet children.
The youngest brother or sister, always handsomest.
And the man who woke up every time Pushkin came by:

*No, I never tire of life,*
*I love life, I want to live,*
*I am no less eager now*
*that I have seen my youth go by.*
*My curiosity still relishes*
*my beloved flights of fancy,*
*every sensation.*

Pushkin's quill flies fast
above the lovelorn rivers.
This isn't literature, because in the sleeping land
even rivers fall in love, and that says something.
And then Tatiana Nikolaevna. Lauaxeta's
drunken sailors and cabin boys, always handsomest.

The wooden table and chairs placed in front
of the grave, to talk and eat with shadows.
A name and two dates.
And if Usolie-Sibiriskoie appeared next to the second date,
how elegant my tombstone would be.
And the man who woke up every time Pushkin came by:

*What does my name mean to you?*
*It is the only reminder,*
*a dead memento on a piece of paper*
*like an epitaph*
*written in strange letters*
*in a language no one understands.*

And then children playing by the shore.
The woman forced to sell her
past and the memory of it.
And the nervous handsomest boy who,
in front of the church of Listvianka, told me
about our earrings and their meaning.
And the man who woke up every time Pushkin came by:

*Bizitzak engainatzen bazaitu*
*ez atsekabetu, ez harrotu,*
*jasan itzazu egun goibelak,*
*alaiagoak helduko dira.*
*Geroan bizi da gure gogoa,*
*gure arima orainak du lotzen.*
*Dena da iheskorra.*
*Etorriko denari ongi etorri.*

Eta gero buriatar guztiak, Ust' Orda-koak,
Aginsk-ekoak eta errepublikakoak,
sorlekua deserri. Mundu zati handi honi
lur lokartua deitu zioten jende ahantziak.
Eta Puxkin agertu ahala esnatu egiten zen gizona:

*Ezin ezabatu lerro tristeak.*

### 66 LERRO HIRI SETIATUAN

Gasteizko plazak eta kaleak lasai zeharkatzean,
egunero bezala lanera edo lagunengana,
bat-batean asaldaturik pentsatzen dut
hau bera han egitea
arriskutsua dela oso egun askotan,
eta etxegainei begiratuz kalkulatzen dut,
begia hotz, dardar gogoa,
zein aukeratuko lukeen franko-tiratzaileak,
nondik etorriko ene burua
lore beltz odolezko bilakatuko duen bala,
susmagarria baita plaza zabalegi hori. Kale hura.
Etxe handiz inguraturiko parkea.

Entzun dut Sarajevoko parkeetan
zuhaitzik ez dagoela jadanik,
biztanleek moztu baitituzte etxeak berotzeko,
eta bat-batean asaldaturik pentsatzen dut
ez dudala nik etxean sua egiteko leku egokirik.
Gainera, ene kalea eraikuntza ofizialez baterik dago,
eta gobernu-bulegoak garrantzizkoak omen direnez
gerra garaian,

*If life betrays you*
*don't get upset, or be arrogant,*
*live through the sadder days*
*because happy ones are ahead.*
*Our mind lives for the morrow,*
*our soul is tied to the now.*
*Everything is ephemeral.*
*Welcome what is to come.*

And then all the opponents, from Ust-Orda,
from Aginsk, from the republic,
all banished from the homeland. All the forgotten people
who named this part of the world the sleeping land.
And the man who woke up every time Pushkin came by:

*I can't delete the sad lines.*


**66 LINES FROM THE CITY UNDER SIEGE**

While leisurely crossing the streets and squares of Gasteiz
like I do every day, to go to work or visit friends,
I realize suddenly, distraught,
that to do this there
is very dangerous most days,
and looking at the roof-tops I try to guess,
with cold eye and tremulous thought,
which one the sniper would choose,
where would the bullet that turns
my head into a black flower come from.
Isn't that square suspiciously wide. And that street.
What about all the tall buildings that surround the park.

I have heard there are no longer
any trees left in the parks of Sarajevo,
that people have used them to heat their houses,
and distraught, I realize suddenly
I couldn't possibly light a fire anywhere in my flat.
And besides, my street is full of official buildings,
and given that government offices are so important
in times of war,

bat-batean asaldaturik pentsatzen dut
kalea istilugune bihurtu eta
suntsiturik egon daitekeela agian
Sarajevoko ene etxea.

Nola moldatzen da ni naizena Sarajevon?
Lanera doa oraindik adibidez? Ala
ohitura arrunt horiek guztiak aspaldian desagertu ziren?
Eta bat-batean asaldaturik pentsatzen dut
ikastetxeak itxita egongo direla ziur asko,
nirea, gainera, trenbidearen bestaldean dagoela, geltokitik hurbil,
eta trenbideak eta geltokiak kontrolatu beharreko gauzak omen direla
gerra garaian.

Luzaro iguriki iristen ez diren eskutitzak
eta berriak ezin izkiriatu.

Nola egiten ditut erosketak Sarajevon?
Kilo patatak hamar marko balio duenetik
orduak ematen ditut batuketak eta kenketak egiten
baina emaitzak gose dira beti.
Eta bat-batean asaldaturik pentsatzen dut
gosea, hotza, izua, ilarak, zori txarra
ohitura ezin arruntegiak direla
gerra garaian.

Banaturik dago jadanik hiria,
barne mugak zauri dira,
eta zauri horien odola ez da metafora,
trenbideaz haraindi etsai lagunak,
zubiaz honaindian lagun etsaiak.
Niri egokitu zaidan egoerari nola egokitu natzaio ni?
Eta bat-batean asaldaturik pentsatzen dut
ama sartaldean bizi dela eta ni berriz erdialdean
eta bi auzoak, anaiarena ere bai, urrunago egon daitezkeela
gerra garaian,
eta banaketa horiek ezustekoak direla eta ankerrak,
gaur hartan zure etxean afaldu nuelako nago hemen.

I realize suddenly, distraught,
that my street might well have turned into a mud field;
my house in Sarajevo
might well have disappeared.

How does my other self in Sarajevo manage?
Does he still go to work, for example? Or
are all those normal habits long gone?
And distraught, I realize suddenly
that the schools are probably closed,
and mine, in any case, is on the other side of the railway line, near the station,
and railway lines and stations are the kind of places that get taken
in times of war.

The long awaited news and letters
I no longer write never reach anywhere.

How do I do the shopping in Sarajevo?
Ever since a kilo of potatoes went up to 10 marks
I spend hours adding and subtracting,
yet the result is always hunger.
And suddenly I realize, distraught,
that hunger, cold, fear, queues, bad luck,
are common currency
in times of war.

And now the city is divided,
its internal borders are wounded,
and the blood oozing from them isn't metaphorical;
from the railway and beyond lie our enemy friends,
from here to the bridge our friendly enemies.
How have I adjusted to the lot that has befallen me?
And distraught, I realize suddenly
that my mother lives in the West and I, unfortunately, in the centre,
and that the two areas, and my brother's too, might be further separated
in times of war,
and that such separations are cruel and unpredictable,
and I will be here then because I ate at yours.

Ez da falta Gasteizko inguruetan
leku egokirik artilleria kokatzeko.
Zaldiaran edo Gasteizko mendiak
ez dira Ilidza mendia bezain ikusgarriak izango,
baina handik jaurtiriko bonbek lan ona egin dezakete.
Eta gero errepideetara oinez irten, pardeltxoak bizkarrean,
hiritar hirigabeak,
udan bada sargori, neguan bada izotz,
inora ez doazen bideetan galdurik,
inon ez dagoen babesaren bila;
bake-itunak sinaru arte bizirik irautea da kontua.
Ez dezala deabruak beste 6 bat idatz.

**EDONON ILARGIA**

Eta hamarrak edo zirelarik
ageri zen ilargia zeruan,
hementxe beste edonon bezala.
Itsasoaren gainean hementxe.
Zuri, handi, dotore sortaldean,
argazkitarako prest.
Alboratuko dute afaria
turista arduratsuek, jakina,
argazkigintzak du lehentasuna
oraintxe beste edonon bezala
ordu desberdinetan –

Japonian egin dituzte jadanik
argazki lainotsuak
tenplu hutsen artean,
betiko mendiaren magalean:
presatiak laboratorioan
lanean emaitzen zain.
Ilargia ilargi.
Ameriketan argazki makinak
prestatzen ari dira gauerako,
egutegian ikusi dute
noiz den – gaur – ilbetea.

The geography of Gasteiz isn't that inappropriate strategically
the artillery would easily find a good place.
Zaldiaran or the mountains of Gasteiz
might not be as spectacular as the Ilid•a range,
but bombs thrown from there can hit targets just as well.
And all the cityless citizens
can go out on the roads on foot with little backpacks too,
and boil in summer and freeze in winter,
get lost on roads that lead nowhere,
and seek a haven that never was;
the key is to stay alive till the peace treaty is signed.
I hope the devil won't add another 6 to that.

**THE MOON ANYWHERE**

Around ten or so
the moon rose in the sky,
right here, like elsewhere.
Above the sea, right here.
White, round, Eastern, elegant,
ready for her photo.
Diligent tourists
interrupt their dinners, no doubt,
because photography is a priority
right now, like elsewhere
a bit later – or earlier.

In Japan, no doubt, shots of
empty temples amidst threadbare clouds
at the foothills of the usual mountains
have been taken already:
someone in a laboratory hurries
to see the results.
The moon the moon.
In America the cameras
are getting ready for the action,
the calendar tells them
tonight is the night: full moon.

Edonon dago leku egoki bat,
hemen itsasoa da,
mendi ubel gorriak,
herrixka bat hondartzan.
Beste edonon bezala hementxe,
hementxe beste edonon bezala.
Ilargia ilargi.
Hondartzaren bukaeran etxe bat,
guztiz bestelakoa,
panpinen bizileku.
Gertaera goibelak ilargitan.

Zaharrek diotenez
gizon arrotz batek zuen eraiki
oso aspaldian alabarentzat,
uste baitzuen hemengo haizeak,
hemengo itsasoak,
senda lezaketela
haurraren gaixotasun hilgarria.
Bai ederra ilargi honen isla
teilatu isilean. Min gordea.
Hementxe beste edonon bezala.
Ezer ez da berri, ezer ez zahar.

Heriotz ahantzi bat
beste mila heriotzen artean.
Ilargi bakar bat
mila ordutan, mila argazkitan
puskaturik, mila begiradatan.
Mila koloreko harri biziek
hatsa digute mindu,
beste edonon bezala hementxe,
non zeru-lurrek Arrieta izen
latitude honetan
bitxia hartu duten.

Perfect places are everywhere,
here it is the sea,
the red and violet mountains,
a little beach town.
Right here like elsewhere,
elsewhere like right here.
The moon the moon.
A house at the end of the beach,
unlike any other,
a dwelling for dolls.
Sad moonlit events.

The story goes
a foreigner built it for his daughter
long, long ago,
because he thought the breeze here,
the sea here,
could cure
her deathly affliction.
How beautiful, this moon's profile
against the quiet roof. A line of pain.
Right here like elsewhere.
Nothing is new, nothing old.

A forgotten death
amongst a thousand other deaths.
A single moon
a thousand moons,
in a thousand photographs,
multiplied before a thousand eyes.
The gemlike patterns of moonlight on rocks
undo me,
right here like elsewhere,
here in this lunar latitude
where earth meets sky,
here
rocky crag.

**ONASSIS TABERNA**

*And, little town, thy streets for evemore,*
*will silent be; and not a soul to tell*
*Why thou art desolate, can e'er return*
John Keats

Orain dela egun pare bat
Zapa kalean nenbilela
taberna baino etxea
genuen zulo ilun hura
suntsiturik ikusi nuen
– aurrera doa hirigintza –.
Hondakinetan sumatzen da
oraindik non zegoen barra,
non komuna, non biltegia,
non banatzen zen zoriona,
nora zeraman eskailerak.
Nik euripean harriturik
pentsatu dut gai ona zela,
erraza eta aproposa,
iragan urrunaren minaz
poema bat izkiriatzeko;
Ponpeia gogora ekarri
adibidez, edo Erroma
– aipuak agian latinez –,
eta poema ederrena
paratu, ele leun ilun,
ubi sunt gaiaren gainean.
Edo, demagun, eskutitz bat,
Fabio lagunari gutuna,
epistola klasikoena,
tabernaren hondamendian
munduarena islatzeko.

Malditismo puntu bat, noski,
beharko luke bukaeran,
Bukovski aipatu, Amsterdam,
kartzela eta heriotza,
eta gainerako guztia.
Baina gero, ene bidea
segitzean – euri gehiegi
hausnarketa poetikoak
atxiki ahal izateko –
pentsatu dut hutsala dela
guztiz joan denaz idaztea,
eta ez dudala gogorik

## ONASSIS TAVERN

*And, little town, thy streets for evermore*
*will silent be; and not a soul to tell*
*Why thou art desolate, can e'er return*
John Keats

A couple of days ago
as I walked down Zapa Street
I saw our favoured dive,
the one that was more home
than bar, being demolished
– call it urban regeneration.
You can still see them, amidst the debris
the contours of the bar,
the toilet, the storeroom,
the corners where joy was dealt,
the shadow of the stairs on a wall.
And in shock, under the rain,
it struck me as a good subject,
both easy and fitting,
for a poem about longing
for a past long gone;
it made me think of Pompeii,
for example, or Rome
– note to self: Latin quotes.
O, to compose the loveliest ode
on the subject of *ubi sunt*
and weave it with wounded words.
Or a letter, say, to Fabio,
my friend; a missive,
a classic epistle like no other,
using the ruins of our bar
to illustrate the fall of civilization.

It'll need an aura of doom,
of course, towards the end,
mention Bukowski, Amsterdam,
jail, death,
and all that.
But, as I walk on
– too much rain
for such
poetic ruminations –
I conclude it's quite vacuous
to write about old stuff,
and I'm not in the mood

iraganaren gorespena
egiteko. Ez baitut inoiz
sinetsi – fedegabe hori –
iragana oraina baino
zoriontsuagoa zenik;
eta jakin, ongi baitakit
zein ondo apaintzen ditugun
atzoko oinaze garratzak,
zein ondo apaintzen ditugun
ustezko zorion zoroak.
Horregatik, kontsideratuz
bizien artean latina
arras ezezaguna dela
– hildakoei berdin zaie –
askoren ustez heroikoak
izan ziren denbora horiek
ahazmenari opa dizkiot
lasai, pena handirik gabe.

**MUSIKAREN LURRALDEAK II**

Kantaidazue Schuberten lied bat,
lied triste bat,
*Malko Euria* edo *Ezki Lorea*,
baso ilunez beterik,
erreka gardenez hanturik,
amodio ezinez gainezka.

Jo ezazue leun pianoa
eta kantaidazue lied tristeena.
Egiozue lekua su bazterrean
Franz gaixoari.

to glorify the past. Because
I have never believed
– heathen that I am –
that we were happier back then,
any more so than today;
and I know, because I know,
how adept we are at
camouflaging the bitter grapes
of yesteryear,
how adept we are at
rehashing imaginary ecstasies.
So. Seeing as how
Latin isn't very *in*
amongst the living
– the dead aren't bothered –
I have gladly offered up
those heroic days
to the gods of forgetfulness.
And, the truth is,
I don't care.

**TERRITORIES OF MUSIC II**

Sing me one of Schubert's Lieder,
one of the sad ones,
*Tränenregen*, or *Der Lindenbaum*,
pregnant with forlorn forests,
swollen with transparent rivers,
brimming with impossible loves.

Play the piano softly
and sing me the saddest Lied.
Make room for poor Franz
by the fire.

Eta *Herz* hitza kantatzea suertatzen bada,
emaiozue behar duen doinu eta keinua
mila zortziehun eta hogeita zazpigarren urteko
erromantikoak baikinan
eta gutarik batek
sendaezinezko gaitz lotsagarria bailuen.
Inork ez baitu inoiz gailenduko
gure ausartzia eta edertasuna.


### ZIN EGITE TELEFONIKOAK

Erreka horiek nola garbitu ezin jakin.
Automobilen artean gogoa galduta
erosketa-poltsekin batera erortzen da
lurrera adorea, inon ez errukirik.
Badoaz usoak sorbaldan pausatzen ziren
garai haiek, haragia soilik izan zena
estatua bilakatu da. Edonon hautsa
eta horbela, ur arreak, leiho goibelak.
Ezagutu dut hemen utzi duzun usaina.
Tronpetak behar ditugu, mesedez, tronpetak.
Zeruari begira hodeien zain geratu
ez euriaren aiduru baizen itzalena.
Kristalaren bestaldean emakumezko bat
begiak malkotan telefonoz hitz egiten,
erosketa-poltsak lurrean barreiaturik;
badirudi bizitza bukatzera doala
baina aurrera doa tamalez geldiezin.
Mendia higatzen duen uraren antzera
higatzen digu gorputza malko bakar batek.

Ba ote dago zin egite telefonikoak baino gauza mingarriagorik?

And if you happen to sing the word *Herz*,
make sure to give it the expression, the modulation it requires,
believe we are Romantics
circa eighteen twenty seven
and one of us has an unmentionable incurable disease.
Because no one will ever comprehend
our courage, our beauty.

## TELEPHONE PROMISES

Impossible to know how to clean those rivers.
Desire is lost amidst the cars;
the last strand of courage collapses on the ground
with the shopping bags, it's no one's fault.
Gone are the days when doves rested on
shoulders, and mere flesh has now
become a statue. Dust and fallen leaves,
murky waters, darkened windows everywhere.
I detect the smell you left behind.
We need trumpets here, please, trumpets.
I stare at the sky waiting for the clouds
and the darkest doesn't harbinger rain.
On the other side of the glass pane
a woman cries as she talks on the phone,
her shopping bags abandoned at her feet;
it feels life is about to end
but it goes on relentlessly, wretched thing.
Rain erodes mountains; likewise,
a single tear corrodes the body, gnaws at it.

Is anything more painful than telephone promises?

## AMODIOZKO POEMA I

Sorginak eta aztiak,
guzti-guztiak bilatu ditut.
Sineskeria orotan
naiz aditua. Amodioa
eskuratzeko asmatu diren
keinu, jolas eta hitzez
artatsu baliatu naiz.
Herrian duzun tradizioa,
Madagaskar urrunetik
datorrena, liburu zaharrek
ilun gordetzen dutena,
dena hartu dut kontuan
zuk jarritako mugen gainetik
ene eskuak hega daitezen.

Zure gorputzak edonon
utzitako hondakinak
bildu ditut. Azkazal zatiak,
erortzen zaizkizun iletxoak,
izardiz blaituriko atorrak,
zure fluido antzuak.
Gero lore bildu berriekin
egosi ditut egunsentian,
harrizko aldareetan erre
artizarra agertzean,
zilarbiziz busti ilargitan,
zure teilatu azpian
sekretuki lurperatu.
Etxearen inguruan
zapi aldiz zazpi bira
egin dut sorginen araoak
ahoan, alkimisten formulak
errepikatu ditut arretaz.

Eta dena une egokian
ongi ezagutzen baitut
izarrek, zu jaiotzean,
atsegin zuten egongunea
Palenkeko horoskopoetan.

**LOVE POEM I**

Witches and soothsayers,
I've researched them all.
I am master of
all superstitions. I have
made careful use of all
gestures, games and words
invented to obtain love.
Even the traditions of your land,
remote Madagascar,
secreted away
in ancient tomes.
All have I taken into account,
so my hands can fly
over the boundaries
you have imposed.

I have collected the leftovers
your body discards everywhere.
Bits of nail, little hairs,
shirts soaked in sweat;
your sterile fluids.
Afterwards I have boiled them
with fresh flowers at dawn,
burnt them on marble altars
under the auspices
of the Morning Star,
drenched them in mercury
under the moonlight,
buried them secretly
under your roof.
Seven times seven turns
I have taken around your house,
chanting fervently meanwhile
the witches' spells,
the alchemists' formulas.

And all at the right times,
because I know the dates
that bode well, according
to the time and place
of your birth
and Palenque's horoscopes.

Baina deusek ez dit balio.
Zure arrazoiak, ilustraziokume hori, indargabetu dizkit sorginkeriak.

Genetikaren baitan jarri dut
orain ene esperantza,
eta berriro hasi naiz
zure hondakinak biltzen.
Azkazal zatiak, iletxoak,
zure fluido antzuak.
Jakintzaleriekin batera
feromonak aztertuko ditut,
aminoazidoak, entzimak,
zure molekula hotzak.
Laster prestatuko dugu
edaberik arrazoizkoena
zuk jarritako mugen gainetik
ene eskuak hega daitezen.

### GILEN AKITANIAKOAK BEZALA

Gilen Akitaniakoak bezala
ezerezez egingo dut poema,
ez nire buruaz, ez besterenaz,
ez amodioaz, ez gaztaroaz,
ezerez hutsez,
esango dut lotan egin dudala
sofan etzanda.

Zein ordutan jaio nintzen ez dakit,
ez naiz atsegin eta ez naiz uzkur,
ez naiz goibel eta ez alegera,
ezin besterik,
ez bada gauez aurkitu nautela
parke batean.

But nothing has worked so far.
Your reason, Renaissance child
that you are,
has weakened my witchcraft.

I have placed my hopes
in genetics now,
and started anew
collecting your leftovers.
Bits of nail, little hairs;
your sterile fluids.
With scientists
I will break down your pheromones,
amino acids, enzymes,
your cold molecules.
Soon we shall have the most
rational of philtres ready,
so my hands can fly
over the boundaries
you have imposed.

## LIKE GILEN OF AQUITAINE

Like Gilen of Aquitaine
I am writing a poem about nothing;
not about me or anyone else
not about love or youth
but about pure nothing.
I will say I had a snooze
on the sofa.

I don't know the time of my birth,
I am not congenial or melancholy,
I am not sad or happy,
and there is nothing else
other than one night, they found me
in a park.

Esaten ez badidate ez dakit
noiz nagoen lotan noiz esnaturik,
bihotz gorria apurtu nahi zidan
min zorrotz batek,
ez nuke zentimorik ordainduko
negarren truke.

Gaixo nago, heriotzaren beldur,
entzun dudana besterik ez dakit,
gustuko medikuren bila nabil,
non egongo den,
sendatzen banau ona izango da,
ez, hiltzen banaiz.

Laguna dut, noski, ez dakit nor den
inoiz ez bainuen inon ikusi,
ez dit onik egin ez txarrik ere,
niri berdin zait,
ez baita inoiz izan lapurtarrik
nire etxean.

Sekula ikusi gabe maite dut,
ez dit baietz esan ez ezetz ere,
ikusten ez badut ez naiz kezkatzen,
begipean dut
beste bat lerdenago, sendoago,
altuagoa.

Ez dakit non bizi den, Berlinen den
ala Parisen, ez, arren, Gasteizen,
ez dut esango egiten didana,
hobe isilik,
hona etortzeko asmorik ez du,
beraz, banoa.

Gilen Akitaniakoak bezala
egin dut poema, ez dakit zertaz,
norbaiten bidez bidaliko diot
beste norbaiti, eraman dezala
azkar Rigara,
eskatuko diot, berak badaki,
giltza gordea.

Unless I am told I never know
whether I am awake or asleep,
a pin-sharp pain
tried to break my red red heart
and I wouldn't pay a penny
for a vessel of tears.

I am sick, afraid of death,
I only know what I have heard,
I'm after a doctor I like
where is he
if he cures me he's fine,
not, however, if I die.

I have a friend, yes, though I ignore who he is,
granted, I've never seen him anywhere,
I've done him no harm or good
and it doesn't matter to me,
for there never was a thief
in my house.

I love him though I have never seen him,
he has never said yes or no
and I don't worry if I don't see him,
I have a handsomer, stronger,
taller one
in reserve.

I ignore where he lives, is it Berlin or
is it Paris; wherever, but please, not Gasteiz,
I won't say what he does to me,
discretion above all,
he has no intention of coming here,
therefore, I am going.

I have written a poem like
Gilen of Aquitaine, I have no idea what it is about,
I will send it to someone through
someone else, please take it over
to Riga soon,
I will ask him, he knows
the secret key.

MIREN AGUR MEABE

PHOTO: ZALDI ERO

MIREN AGUR MEABE was born in Lekeitio in 1962. She is a qualified teacher and has a degree in Basque philology. She taught at a Basque school (*ikastola*) in Bilbao for some years, but since 1992 she has been an editor at the Giltza-Edebé publishing house where she is now Senior Editor.

Meabe has received many prizes, amongst others the 1991 Lasarte-Oria Poetry Prize for the collection *Oi, ondarrezko emakaitz!* (Oh, Wild Woman of Sand!), the 1997 Imagina Ezazu Euskadi prize for the volume *Ohar Orokorrak* (General Notes), the 2001 Spanish Critics' Prize for the collection *Azalaren Kodea* (The Code of the Skin), and the 2002 Euskadi prize for *Itsalabarreko etxea* (The Cliff House).

She writes mostly poetry, children's and young people's literature and short stories. Her first publication was the short story collection *Uneka... gaba* (Momentarily... Night) and in 2000 she edited a collection of short stories by twenty-nine Basque women writers entitled *Gutiziak* (Desire). She has also translated a number of children's books into Basque.

Her poems have been translated into several languages and published internationally in magazines and anthologies and she has appeared in many European literary events and festivals.

**KODEA**

Bestelako kodea aldarrikatu nahi dut:
hitzarena ez bezalako kodea,
hizkera ez-hitzezkoa,
oroimenean kondenatu ezineko lengoaia,
zinak gezurta ditzakeen berbakera,
erreklamazio-libururik eta
tarifa-zerrendarik gabeko mintzo mutua,
mezu anbiguoz itxuraturiko jario askea,
adierazi gura ez denaren adierazpidea.

**MEMORIA EZ GALTZEKO OHARRAK (2)**

Zabalik utzi nuen bart logelako leihoa
eta piztia bat sartu zen.
Aireari usnaka zebilen:
uste dut igarri ninduela izara artean kuzkurtuta.
Ez zekien biluzik nengoena, bere zain,
ezta bere izena nekienik ere.
Animalia ugaztuna zen,
burusoildua,
bularrean bilo gutxikoa,
ipurdi irtenekoa,
begiak kilometroz eta loguraz beterik
eta tabako, kresal eta ogitarteko hotzen nahastea
ahoan.

Adurra erori zitzaion alfonbra gainera,
eta infernuko itsasoen moduan
hasi zen zorua txinpartaka.
Alboetara behatu zuen,
eta lokatzezko hilobi baten moduan
desitxuratu ziren hormak.
Bizkarrean egin zuen hazka,
eta nire bularrak puztu egin ziren
mundua udaberrian ohi den legez.

Egia diot.

**CODE**

I proclaim an alternative code:
unrelated to words,
a language without phrases,
a tongue that cannot be condemned to memory,
a prose to fool promises,
a mute dialect with no
price-lists or complaint forms,
a free fountain of ambiguous meanings,
a way to express all that cannot be expressed.

**NOTES ON HOW TO AVOID MEMORY LOSS (2)**

I left the bedroom window open last night
and a beast entered.
It sniffed the air:
I think it sensed me curled between the sheets.
It never guessed I was naked, waiting,
nor that I knew its name.
It was a mammal, this creature,
grown bald,
with sparse fuzz on its chest,
and round, pert buttocks,
eyes full of sleep and the horizon,
and a mixture of sea salt, tobacco and
bread gone slightly stale on its breath.

It dribbled froth all over the carpet,
and like a hell-bound ocean,
the fool started to spit and crackle,
looked right and left
and the walls gave way
like tombstones moulded in mud.
It scratched one shoulder
and my breasts billowed
like the world in springtime.

I swear.

**OHAR LABURRAK (1)**

Atzo izara bat erre zitzaidan.
Erre egin nuen lisaburdinaz.
Ogi xigortuaren koloreko triangelua estanpatu nion
telebistaren erruz.
Beti izaten dut piztuta sukaldeko telebista txikia
arropa lisatu behar dudanean:
gerrako haurtxo beltz bat
ama hilaren titia miazkatzen ari zen.
Ilezko korapiloa egin zitzaidan eztarrian.

Ez zait ahaztuko,
esneak sujetadorea umeldu zidan eta.



\*\*\*


Bildu nire igitai-ilargi izoztuaren jario zurbila,
nire platinozko sexuaren lurrin azukretua.
Oratu nire gerri suminduaren bihurgune ahazkorra.
Biribildu nire bular iraunkorraren obalo goibela,
zure aho-errotarriaz eho bularmutur mingotsa.
Txoriarrainek albokera erortzen ikus gaitzaten arte,
zure txistu-haziak nire ezpainetan haize bihurtu artio.

**BRIEF NOTES (1)**

Yesterday I burnt a sheet,
with the iron,
did it myself,
embossed a burnt-toast coloured triangle on it
thanks to the TV.
I always keep the small TV on in the kitchen
when ironing looms:
a black child from a war
suckled his dead mother's breast.
I felt I'd swallowed a ball of hair.
I won't forget it:
milk seeped into my bra.


\*\*\*


Scoop the pale flow of my frozen half-moon,
the sweet syrup of my platinum sex.
Knead the dormant curve of my burning waist,
cup the sad oval of my perennial breast,
grind my bitter nipples with your mouth.
Until flying fish witness our sideways fall
and semen and saliva evaporate from my lips.

**GALDEKETA**

Non daude pozaldi horailetatik
batzeko ginen taupada hordigarri haiek?
Non, belaontzien ezpalez
eraikitzekotan ginen sutondo ibiltaria?
Non dago tigreen marrekin
dekoratu nahi genuen aberri berria?
Non, iraganaren magalari atximurka eginez
berretsi gura genituen gure paisajeak?
Non da lehen ohe hartako erloju ezberdina?
Non galdu dugu misterioaren ura,
zeinahi utopia bedeinkatzeko balio ziguna?
Non gorde duzu irudimenaren maleta?
Zer dago orain barruan?


***


Basalarrosek miazkatu dute
baselizaren zurezko arkupea.
Hantxe, harrizko murruaren kontra
amodioa antzeztu genuen aspaldiko arrasti hartan.
Euriak zelaiari erauzten zion busti-hotsa
zeure hatzek atera zioten nire sexuari.
Armiarma-sarean zehar ostadarra ikusten nuen
zuk bultza eta bultza
ezerezaren kontra egiten zenidan bitartean.
Gero, trinki-tranka aldendu ginen errepidean aurrera
gorputzei bihozminaren salda epela zeriela.
Huraxe izan zen atzen enkontruetako bat,
gure azal umelak ordurako bazekielarik
elkarrentzat ez ginela.

## QUESTIONS

Where did they go,
the delirious heartbeats
we said we'd gather as we laughed back then?
Where the portable home
we said we'd build out of ships' carcasses?
Where the new nation
we would decorate with tiger stripes?
Where the landscape we said we'd rob
from the hidey-hole of the past?
Where did that special clock we kept by our first bed go?
Where did we lose the water of mysteries
with which we blessed so many Utopias?
Where did you put the suitcase of the imagination?
What do you keep there now?

\*\*\*

Wild roses have gobbled up
the latticed arch in front of the hermitage.
It was there, against the stone wall,
that we made love that afternoon.
The rain dispersed the meadow's cool dampness
as your fingers reconjured it from my sex.
I could see a rainbow on a spider's web
as you rammed and rammed
fighting my body against the void.
Later, we gracelessly lost each other on the path,
our bodies still dripping with the lukewarm soup of heartbreak.
That, in short, was one of our most definitive encounters,
our ripe flesh aware by then
we weren't made for each other.

## GAUZA KONKRETUAK

Sukaldean jarrita nago, makarroiak egosi bitartean.

Gauza konkretuak maite ditut
eta horien izenak errepasatzea gosaldu baino lehen:
iratzargailua, euria kalean, supermerkatua,
musuak siestan,
ardo bat, koadrila,
semearen esku ttipiak,
jendea plazan,
zu...

Kilima gozo-gozoak egiten dizkidate,
dieta ostean oturuntzak egiten dituenaren antzekoak.
Ezinezkoa zait eguneroko gauza horietatik aldentzea:
boligrafoetara itsatsi zaizkit eta ez dakit astintzen.

Dena den,
gauza konkretuek ez dute luzapenik onartzen:
makarroiak egosita daude dagoeneko.
Bizimodua honelakoxea da.
Poema baten germena hozitzen hasten denerako,
badator egunerokotasuna sakaka.
Eta mahaitik jaiki beharra,
ernegu lirdingatsu baten menpe.

**CONCRETE THINGS**

I am sitting in the kitchen, while the pasta boils.

I love concrete things
to learn their names before breakfast:
alarm clock, rain on the pavement, supermarket,
siesta kisses,
a glass of wine, friends,
my son's small hands,
people in the square,
you…

They produce the sweetest, most languorous tickles,
like a sybaritic feast after a fast.
I find it impossible to turn from such things:
they've stuck to my pen and I can't seem to shake them off.

But nevertheless,
concrete things won't allow delays,
and the pasta is ready now.
Such is life.
Just when the seedling of a poem starts to germinate,
there comes the mundane barging in.
And I have to get up from the table,
as shades of a bilious mood settle.

**INURRIA (II)**

Nire bertuteak, noizbehinka haren berri izatearen truke:
dei bat,
irudi lauso bat ispiluan,
edozer telekinesiaz mugitzen.

Larunbatero joaten naiz kanposantura.
Egun on – esaten diot –, neu naiz, inurria.
Loreak eta hitzak,
kristal-papurrak,
hauts-eskukadak ekarri dizkizut.

Lixaz karrakatzen dut euriak erdituriko liken horizta.
Etzan, eta marmolezko izenak musukatzen.

Hodeiek gorantz urrupatzen naute;
harriek beherantz xurgatzen.
Odolezko hariak daude belarretan.
Hilobiaren alde banatan,
Ilargia eta Eguzkia
neuri begira.

**AMETSETAKO URAK (III)**

Ura telefonoan zure ahotsa.
Edalontzi bat dago mesillan.
Hari begira hartzen nau loak.
Ohea urak hartzen du.
Kamisoia blai, banoa
itsasargi baten pareraino,
non zu zauden, niri mail bat idazten.
Subject: "Ura, mesedez."
(Nire ahotsa ba ote da zuretzat ura?)
Begiak ireki ditut. Eskua luzatu dut. Edalontzia jausi da.
Kristalek, zoruan, zure izena dioste.
Bustita esnatu naiz.

**THE ANT (II)**

My riches in exchange for some contact:
a call,
a fleeting face in a mirror,
things afloat telekinetically.

I go to the cemetery on Saturdays.
Good morning – I tell her – it's me, the ant.
Here, I brought you words and flowers,
shreds of glass,
handfuls of dust.

I scrape yellowy crusts of lichen, rain bequests, with my nail file.
I lie down and cover the marble letters with kisses.

Clouds drag me up;
rocks pull me down.
I see threads of blood in blades of grass.
Right and left
the moon and sun
watch me.

**WATER DREAMS (III)**

Your voice on the phone is water.
A glass on the side table.
I fall asleep looking at it.
Water floods the bed.
My nightdress swells, I drift
towards a lighthouse,
where you happen to be,
writing an email to me.
*Subject:* "Water, please."
(Is my voice water to you?)
I open my eyes. I stretch my arm out. The glass falls.
The pieces on the ground spell your name.
I wake up wet.

**EOLIA(III)**

Mitoak dio Eolia fruituz eta lorez beterik zegoela.
Hostotsu irudikatzen dut uharte hori, nire…
– nire pubisa bezala esateko nintzen,
baina nire pubisa mehetu da eta nire bular-muturrak ere zurbildu
dira –.
Badakigu, poeta jakintsuaren arabera,
uharteak bidaiatu egiten zuela,
eta horregatik inork ezin zuela hara berriz itzuli.
Ni ere banaiz Eolia antzeko bat, taupadaka.
Hala ere, irrikaz nago aurki nazazun,
betazalak bioletaz apaindurik
eta ahoa zure gustuko esaldiz.

Oreka galtzen dut. Ez duenari zentzua bilatzen diot. Oker dihardut.
Ez naiz Eolia eta ez nabil ihesi.
Zu ez zara nire taupadaz elikatzen,
zuk ibilitako urak ez dira hauek berberak.

**AEOLIA (III)**

According to the myth Aeolia was full of fruits and flowers.
I imagine a luxuriant island, like my...
I was going to say like my pubis,
but my pubis is sparse now and my nipples pale.

We know, because the ancients told us,
that the island travelled the seas,
and hence no one could ever return to it.
Me too, I am a kind of Aeolia, and I pulsate
and long for you to find me
and beautify my eyelids with violets
and my mouth with the words you love.

I have lost control. I make sense of the senseless. I am wrong.
I am not Aeolia nor am I wandering.
You are not nourished by my pulse,
these are not the waters you navigate.

**KIRMEN URIBE**

PHOTO: TXOMIN SAEZ

KIRMEN URIBE was born in Ondarroa in 1970 and belongs to the first generation of writers whose whole schooling, from kindergarten to university, was conducted entirely in Basque. He holds a degree in Basque philology and has done postgraduate courses on Literary Theory and Comparative Literature at the University of Trento, in Italy. He has translated poems by authors such as Raymond Carver, Sylvia Plath and Mahmud Darwish into Basque.

He is more widely known as a poet, but has also written books for children. His poems have been translated into several languages and published in international magazines such as the American *New Yorker, Circumference* and *Open City* and the Berlin-based poetry portal *Lyrikline*. He has taken part in many international events in Europe and North America, and has given talks at universities in New York, Barcelona and Madrid.

He has taken part in many multimedia projects and made video poems too. In 2003, together with three Basque musicians and an artist he set in motion the project *Zaharregia, txikiegia agian. Una manera de mirar.* (Too old, too small, maybe) bringing out a CD and performing in New York, San Francisco, Munich, Berlin, Barcelona and Ireland.

Uribe has worked in the cinema, and is writing his first novel.

**IBAIA**

Garai batean ibaia zen hemen
baldosak eta bankuak dauden tokian.
Dozena bat ibai baino gehiago daude hiriaren azpian,
zaharrenei kasu eginez gero.
Orain langile auzo bateko plaza besterik ez da.
Eta hiru makal dira ibaiak hor
azpian jarraitzen duen seinale bakar.

Denok dugu barruan uhola dakarren ibai estali bat.
Ez badira beldurrak, damuak dira.
Ez badira zalantzak, ezinak.

Mendebaleko haizeak astintzen ditu makalak.
Nekez egiten du oinez jendeak.
Laugarren pisuan emakume nagusi bat
leihotik arropak botatzen ari da:
alkandora beltza bota du eta gona kuadroduna
eta zetazko zapi horia eta galtzerdiak
eta herritik iritsi zen neguko egun hartan
soinean zeramatzan txarolezko zapata zuribeltzak.
Hegabera izoztuak ematen zuten bere oinek elurretan.

Haurrak arropen atzetik joan dira arineketan.
Ezkontzako soinekoa atera du azkenik,
makal batean pausatu da baldar,
txori pisuegi bat balitz bezala.

Zarata handi bat entzun da. Izutu egin dira oinezkoak.
Haizeak errotik atera du makaletako bat.
Zuhaitzaren erroek emakume nagusi baten eskua dirudite,
beste esku batek noiz laztanduko zain.

**THE RIVER**

There was a river here once
where the paving stones and the benches are.
More than a dozen rivers flow under the city
they say.
This is now a square in a working class area.
Three poplars the only sign
of the river's presence underneath.

We all carry a hidden river ready to rise.
With fear or regret.
With doubt or anger.

The westerly wind lashes at the poplars.
People can hardly walk.
On the fourth floor an old woman
throws clothes out of the window:
a black shirt and a chequered skirt,
a yellow silk scarf and a pair of tights
and the two-tone patent leather shoes
she wore the day she arrived in town.
They look like two frozen lapwings on the snow.

Children chase after the floating clothes.
Her wedding dress flies out last
and pauses gracelessly on a poplar branch,
like a bird grown too fat.
A big crash. People shout and run.
The wind has torn a poplar from the ground.
Its roots an upturned hand
that wants to be touched.

**IRLA**

*Horixe da zoriona,*
*orduka lan egiten duen behargina.*
Anne Sexton

Igandea da hondartzan asmo oneko jendearentzat.
Hango harrabots urruna entzuten da irlatik.

Uretara sartu gara biluzik,
Anemonak, trikuak, barbarinak ikusi ditugu hondoan.
Begira, haizeak garia bezala mugitzen du urak hondarra.
Urpera sartu eta azpitik begiratu zaitut.
Atsegin dut esku eta zangoen mugimendu geldoa,
Atsegin sabelpeak itsasbelarren forma hartzean.

Lehorrera igo gara. Bero da eta itzal egiten dute pinuek.
Gaziak dira zure besoak, gazia bularra, sabela gazia.
Ilargia itsasoarekin lotzen duen indar berak
lotu gaitu geu ere.
Mendeak segundo bihurtu dira eta segundoak mende.
Udare zurituak gure gorputzak.

Anemonak, trikuak, barbarinak ikusi ditugu hondoan.
Igandea da hondartzan asmo oneko jendearentzat.

**BISITA**

Heroina larrua jotzea bezain gozoa zela
esaten zuen garai batean.

Medikuek esaten dute okerrera ez duela egin,
eguna joan eguna etorri, eta lasai hartzeko.
Hilabetea da berriro esnatu ez dela
azken ebakuntzaz geroztik.

Hala ere egunero egiten diogu bisita
Arreta Intentsiboko Unitateko seigarren kutxara.
Aurreko oheko gaisoa negar batean aurkitu dugu gaur,
inor ez zaiola bisitara agertu diotso erizainari.

## THE ISLAND

*So this is happiness,*
*that journeyman.*
Anne Sexton

Sunday at the beach for all people of goodwill.
Distant ruckus from the island.

We enter the water naked,
and watch anemones, mullets and sea urchins on the rocky bottom.
Look, a field of wheat swaying in the wind down there.
I dive and observe you from below.
I love the lazy motions of your hands and feet,
I love it that your sex is like algae.

We go back to dry land. It's hot, the pine woods offer shade.
Your arms are salty; like your nipples, salty; and your belly, salty too.
The force that binds moon and sea binds us too.
Centuries turn into seconds, seconds into centuries.
The pear-white flesh of your body.

We watch the anemones, mullets and sea urchins on the rocky bottom.
Sunday at the beach for all people of goodwill.

## THE VISIT

I remember her saying heroin felt as good as sex
some time ago.

The doctors say she is no worse,
and to take things as they come, one day at a time.
It's been a month since she last woke,
after the operation.

But we visit her daily anyway,
in bed six in the Intensive Care Unit.
The patient across from her is inconsolable when we arrive,
she cries to the nurse, no one came today.

Hilabetea arrebaren hitzik entzun ez dugula.
Ez dut lehen bezala bizitza osoa aurretik ikusten,
esaten zigun,
ez dut promesarik nahi, ez dut damurik nahi,
maitasun keinu bat besterik ez.

Amak eta biok soilik hitz egiten diogu.
Anaiak lehen ez zion gauza handirik esaten,
orain ez da agertu ere egiten.
Aita atean geratzen da, isilik.

Ez dut gauez lorik egiten, esaten zigun arrebak,
beldur diot loak hartzeari, beldur amesgaiztoei.
Orratzek min egiten didate eta hotz naiz,
hotza zabaltzen dit sueroak zainetan zehar.

Gorputz ustel honi ihes egingo banio.

Bitartean heldu eskutik, eskatzen zigun,
ez dut promesarik nahi, ez dut damurik nahi,
maitasun keinu bat besterik ez.

**MAHMUD**

Aipa nezake lehenik ama, Assia arreba gaztea,
eta Aita, besamotza eta edadetua, etxeko patioan.
Aipa nitzake zerurik zabalenak, albaraka lurrina,
laranja urez bustitako eskuak.

Aipa nezake Kotimo, lagunik minena, handia eta umoretsua.
Nola ikusten genuen telebista elkarrekin,
nola egiten genuen eskolak ihesi Tangerreko molletara joateko,
nola imajinatzen genituen Londres, Amsterdam edo New York,
portuko urazalaren gasolina orbanetan.

Bada behin eta berriz entzun dudan kontakizun bat.
Aitak kontatzen zigun txikitan.
Toledo izeneko hiri bat aipatzen zuen,
bazela hiri hartan dorre bat,
eta dorrean ate bat hogeita lau giltzarrapoz kondenatua.

It's been a month since we heard my sister's voice.
I don't see my life ahead of me as I used to,
she said,
I don't want promises, I don't want remorse,
just show me love.

Only my mother and I talk to her.
My brother never said much,
now he won't even turn up.
My father leans silently in the doorway.

I don't sleep at night, my sister said,
I am afraid of sleep, of the nightmares.
The needles hurt and I am cold,
the serum seeps cold through my veins.

I wish I could escape this useless body.

Hold my hand awhile, she said,
I don't want promises, I don't want remorse,
just show me love.


**MAHMUD**

I could start with my mother, or my youngest sister, Assia,
and my father – elderly, one-armed, in the courtyard.
I could mention the wideness of the skies, the scent of basil,
the hands wet with orange juice.

I could mention Kotimo, my best friend, so big and cheerful.
And how we watched TV together,
how we used to skive off school to go to the pier in Tangier,
how we pictured London, Amsterdam or New York
on the oil-stained sea water of the port.

There is a story I heard over and over again.
Father used to tell us when we were kids
about a city named Toledo
and how there was a tower there,
and in the tower, a door secured with twenty-four padlocks.

Kontatzen zigun errege bat hil bakoitzean
beste giltzarrapo bat jartzen zuela errege berriak,
aurrekoen ohiturari jarraituz.
Hogeita bosgarren erregeari jakinminak gehiago egin zion,
eta erreinuko jakintsuen esanei muzin eginez
giltzarrapoak banan banan kendu eta atea zabaltzeko agindu zuen.
Mundu guztiaren harridurarako,
dorre barruan margo batzuk besterik ez zituzten aurkitu.
Horixe zen hango altxor guztia.
Margoek soldadu arabeak irudikatzen zituzten, zaldiak, gameluak.
Eta azken margoan gaztigu hau:
ate hau zabaltzean soldadu arabeek hartuko dute hiria.

Ilundu orduko sartu zen Tariq b. Ziyad Toledoko hirian,
eta berehala hil zuen bertako erregea,
jakinminak gehiago egin zion errege hura.

Aitaren kontakizuna nuen gogoan Tangerretik Cadizerako bidean.
Europako gerra batean galdu zuen besoa aitak.
Esaten zuen ez zegoela ezer itsasoaz bestalde,
kentzeko asmo horiek burutik, zahar sentitzen zela,
laguntza behar zutela etxea gobernatzeko.

Aipa nezake gauez atera ginela Tangerretik,
hogeita lau ordu luze behar izan genituela Cadizera heltzeko.
Aipa nezake ehun eta berrogeita hamar mila
kobratu zigula patroiak bidaiaren truke.
Eta berrogei gehiago, poliziak ikusi gabe
hondartzatik aterako gintuela agindu zigun alproja hark,
dirua hartu baina gure bila agertu ez zen berak.

Gero etorri ziren Madril, Bartzelona, Bordele, Bilbo.
Eraikinak, denda handiak, galsoro lehorrak.
Baita gaua eta alkohola ere
eta pikuak bezala urtzen ziren gorputz lirainak.

Bada behin eta berriz burura datorkidan amesgaizto bat,
amesgaiztorik latzena. Benetan jazoriko horiek baitira latzenak.
Ezin ahantz dezaket Kotimo, liskar batean hila
hondartzako alproja harekin topo egin ondoren.
Zorigaitzaren kontuak.
Ezin ahantz, berrogei mila horiengatik
egin zutela bat komun hartan odolak eta elurrak.

He told us how every time a king died
the new king would add another padlock
to continue the custom of his predecessors.
But the twenty-fifth king was so curious
he disregarded the advice of all the wise men of the kingdom
and ordered the padlocks be removed one by one and the door opened.
To everyone's surprise,
all they found in the tower were some paintings.
No other treasures were found.
The paintings depicted Arab soldiers, horses, camels.
The last one this prophecy:
the day the door opens Arab soldiers will take the city.

Before nightfall Tariq bin Ziyad had entered the city
and slain its king there and then,
that king who was so curious.

I thought of my father's story on the way from Tangier to Cadiz.
He had lost his arm in a European war.
He said there was nothing on the other side of the sea,
to forget all that nonsense, that he felt old
and needed help around the house.

I could mention that we left Tangier at night,
that we took twenty-four long hours getting to Cadiz.
I could mention that the pilot charged us
one hundred and fifty thousand for the journey.
And forty more we paid the bastard who promised
to get us off the beach unseen by police and never came.

After that: Madrid, Barcelona, Bordeaux, Bilbao.
Buildings, big shops, yellow wheat fields.
And nights and alcohol too,
and fragile bodies that melted like soft figs.

I have this recurring nightmare that won't leave me,
one of the worst kind. The kind that really happened, the worst kind.
I can't forget Kotimo, dead in a fight.
We met the bastard who never came to the beach.
Bad luck is what it was.
For the sake of forty thousand
blood melted into snow in that lavatory.

Patioan utzi ditut lagunak. Galerietarantz egin dut.
Urrun da albaraka lurrina, urrun laranja-urez bustiriko eskuak.
Burdinazko ateak zeharkatzen ari da labanderiako gurditxoa.
Begira egoten naiz horrelakoetan.
Barrote artetik kaleko atea ere ikusten dut suerterik bada.
Ongi zenbatuak ditut hemendik kalera dauden ateak.

Hogeita lau giltzarrapo besterik ez dira.

#### KUKUA

Apirilaren hasieran entzun zuen aurrena kukua.
Urduri zebilelako beharbada,
kaosa ordenatzeko joera horrengatik beharbada,
kukuak zein notatan kantatzen zuen jakin nahi izan zuen.

Hurrengo arratsaldean, hantxe egon zen basoan zain,
diapasoia eskuan, kukuak noiz kantatuko.
Diapasoiak ez zioen gezurrik.
Si-sol ziren kukuaren notak.

Aurkikuntzak bazterrak astindu zituen.
Mundu guztiak frogatu nahi zuen benetan
nota horietan kantatzen ote zuen kukuak.
Baina neurketak ez zetozen bat.
Bakoitzak bere egia zuen.
Fa-re zirela zioen batek, Mi-do besteak.
Ez ziren ados jartzen.

Bitartean, kukuak kantari jarraitzen zuen basoan:
ez si-sol, ez fa-re, mi-do ezta ere.
Mila urte lehenago bezala,
kukuak kuku, kuku kantatzen zuen.

I leave my friends in the courtyard. I head towards the gallery above.
The scent of basil is far away, like the hands wet with orange juice.
The laundry trolley passes through the iron doors.
I often watch this happen.
If I am lucky I can see the door to the street through the bars.
I have counted and recounted the number of doors.

Only twenty-four puny padlocks.


## THE CUCKOO

It was the beginning of April when he first heard the cuckoo.
And maybe because he was stressed,
or because of his tendency to subdue chaos,
he wanted to know the notes the cuckoo sang.

The next evening he was in the forest, ready,
tuning fork in hand, waiting for the cuckoo to sing.
The tuning fork didn't lie.
The cuckoo sang ti-do.

The discovery sent shock waves all around.
Everybody wanted to check if the cuckoo
really sang those notes.
But there were conflicting assessments.
Different people believed different things.
Someone said it was fa-so, someone else la-ti.
They couldn't agree.

Meanwhile the cuckoo kept singing in the forest:
It wasn't ti-do, la-ti or fa-so.
Like a thousand years ago,
just cuckoo, cuckoo.

**TXORIAK NEGUAN**

Txoriak salbatzea zen gure misioa.
Elurretan preso geratu ziren txoriak salbatzea.

Hondartza aldean egoten ziren gordeta gehienak
        itsaso beltzaren abarora.
Txoriak ere beltzak ziren.
Babeslekutik atera eta etxera eramaten genituen
        patrikaretan sartuta.
Txori txiki-txikiak, gure haur eskuetan ere
        doi-doi sartzen zirela.

Gero, berogailuaren ondoan jartzen genituen.
Txoriek baina ez zuten luzaroan irauten.
Bi edo hiru orduren buruan hil egiten ziren.
Guk ez genuen ulertzen zergatik,
ez genuen ulertzen haien esker txarra.
Izan ere, esnetan bustitako ogi apurrak ematen genizkien
        jatera ahora
eta ohea ere prestatzen genien
gure bufandarik koloretsuenekin.

Alferrik baina, hil egiten ziren.

Gurasoek haserre, esaten ziguten
ez ekartzeko txori gehiago etxera,
hil egiten zirela gehiegizko beroagatik.
Eta natura jakintsua dela
iritsiko zela udaberria bere txoriekin.

Gu pentsakor jartzen ginen une batez,
beharbada gurasoak zuzen izango dira.

Hala eta guztiz ere,
biharamonean berriro joango ginen hondartza aldera
        txoriak salbatzera.
Gure ahalegina
itsasoan elurra bezain alferrekoa zela jakin arren.

Eta txoriek hiltzen jarraitzen zuten, txoriek hiltzen.

**BIRDS IN WINTER**

Our mission was to save the birds.
The birds imprisoned in the snow.

Most took refuge near the beach
      where they sheltered from the black sea.
The birds were black too.
We dug them from their hideaway and brought them home
      in our pockets.
The birds were very very small, and fitted snugly
      in our tiny tiny hands.

Afterwards we placed them near the stove.
The birds, however, never lasted long.
They'd be dead after two hours or three.
We didn't understand why,
we didn't understand their lack of gratitude.
Considering we fed milk-sodden bread crumbs
      into their beaks,
considering we built beds for them
with our most colourful scarves.

All in vain, they always died.

We angered our parents, they told us
never to bring birds home again,
that they died of excessive heat.
That nature is wise
and spring would bring more birds.

We would consider this for a while,
thinking our parents might well be right.

But despite this
the following day we'd descend on the beach again,
      to save more birds.
Even though we knew
      our efforts were as pointless as snow on the sea.

And the birds died, relentlessly they died.

**GAUZA PERFEKTUAK**

Oinentzat mesede izan arren, zapatentzat
sandaliek eskeletoen antza dute.
Olibondoak bi mila urte betetzen ditu
baina ez da ezertaz gogoratzen.

Gauza perfektuek ikara sortzen didate.
Ez ditut atsegin.
Nire letra okerra da, pausua okerragoa,
egin ahalak egin.

**EZIN ESAN**

Ezin da esan Libertatea, ezin da esan Berdintasuna,
ezin da esan Anaitasuna, ezin esan.
Ez zuhaitz ez erreka ez bihotz.
Ahaztu egin da antzinako legea.

Uholak eraman du hitzen eta gauzen arteko zubia.
Ezin zaio esan tiranoak erabaki irizten dionari heriotz.
Ezin da esan norbait falta dugunean,
oroitzapen txikienak odolusten gaituenean.

Inperfektua da hizkuntza, higatu egin dira zeinuak
errotarri zaharrak bezala, ibiliaren ibiliz. Horregatik,

ezin da esan Maitasuna, ezin da esan Edertasuna,
ezin da esan Elkartasuna, ezin esan.
Ez zuhaitz ez erreka ez bihotz.
Ahaztu egin da antzinako legea.

Alabaina "ene maitea" zure ahotik entzutean
aitor dut zirrara eragiten didala,
dela egia, dela gezurra.

**PERFECT THINGS**

They make feet content, but shoes
think sandals look much like skeletons.
This olive tree will be two thousand years old soon,
but can't remember a thing.

Perfect things scare me.
I don't like them.
My writing is crooked, so is my posture,
try as I might.


**THE UNSAYABLE**

You can't say Liberty, you can't say Equality,
you can't say Fraternity; can't say it.
Can't say tree or river or heart.
Old laws no longer apply.

Floods have washed away the bridge between words and things.
You can't say a despot's decision is murder.
You can't say you miss someone
if a mundane memory pricks your soul.

Language is imperfect, signs are eroded
like old millstones that turn and turn too long. And so,

you can't say Love, you can't say Beauty,
you can't say Solidarity; can't say it.
Can't say tree or river or heart.
Old laws no longer apply.

But still, I confess that when I hear you
say "my love" I feel electric,
be it truth, be it lie.

**APARTE-APARTEAN**

Sei urterekin egin zuten lehen itsasoratzea aitak eta osabak,
eta patroitza Bustio baporean ikasi.
Gogorrak ziren garai hartako patroiak,

ekaitz egunetan ukabilak estutu eta zerura begira
"bizarrik badaukazu etorri hona!"
Jainkoari amenazu egiten zieten horietakoak.

Mutil koskorrak zirenean, igandeko mezetara
txandaka joan behar izaten zuten lau anai nagusiek,
traje bakarra baitzen etxean. Bata elizatik etorri,

trajea erantzi, besteari eman
eta horrela joaten ziren mezetara,
nor bere orduan, nor bere zapatez.

Umetan, aita itsasotik iristen zen egunean,
portuko morro luzeenean egoten ginen zain
mendebaldera begira. Hasieran

ezer ikusten ez bazen ere, laster
antzematen zuen gutariko batek hodeiertzean
puntu beltz bat, pixkanaka itsasontzi bilakatzen zena.

Ordu beteren buruan heltzen zen ontzia morrora,
eta bira egiten zuen gure aurrean portura sartzeko.
Aitak agur egiten zigun eskuaz.

Ontzia igaro orduko, ariniketan joaten ginen
atrakatu behar zuten tokira.
Aita ohean azkenetan zegoela ere

gorazarre egiten zion bizitzari,
eguna bizi behar dela esaten zigun,
beti arduratuta ibiliz gero ihes dagiela bizitzak.

Eta agintzen zuen: Beti iparralderago
joan behar duzue, ez da sarea bota behar
arraina ziur dagoela dakizuen tokian,

aparte-apartean bilatu behar da,
daukazuenarekin konformatu gabe.
"Heriotzak ez du irabaziko",

**WAY BEYOND**

Aged six my father and uncle first went to sea,
and learnt to pilot at the Bustio.
That was a generation of tough men.

On stormy days they shook their fists at the sky
"come down here if you have the balls!"
They weren't afraid to threaten God.

As young lads the eldest four
took turns to attend Sunday mass,
and share a single suit. One took

the suit off and passed it to the next,
and that's how they went to mass,
one at a time, each with his own shoes.

When I was a kid, on the days father came ashore
we waited at the tip of the breakwater,
eyes firmly on the West. Maybe at first

we didn't see much, but after a while
one of us would spot a black dot emerging
from the horizon, a dot that became ship.

After an hour the ship reached the breakwater
and turned in front of us to enter the port.
Father waved his hand.

We ran to their mooring bollard
to be there before they arrived.
Even near the end, in bed by then,

father praised the beauty of life,
he said we ought to savour every day,
that worrying only kept life at bay.

And he commanded: always go
further north, never throw your net
where you know the catch to be,

you must aim way beyond,
don't be content with certainty.
"And death shall have no dominion",

idatzi zuen Dylan Thomasek,
baina nonoiz irabazten du,
eta halaxe amatatu zen aitaren bizitza ere,

mendebaldera eginez
hodeiertzean galtzen zen itsasontzia bezala,
uberan oroitzapenak marraztuz.

**MAIATZA**
*Utzi begietara begiratzen.*
*Nola zauden jakin nahi dut.*
       Rainer W. Fassbinder

Begira, sartu da maiatza,
Zabaldu du bere betazal urdina portuan.
Erdu, aspaldian ez dut zure berri izan,
Ikarati zabiltza, ito ditugun katakumeak bezala.
Erdu eta egingo dugu berba betiko kontuez,
Atsegin izatearen balioaz,
Zalantzekin moldatu beharraz,
Barruan ditugun zuloak nola bete.
Erdu, sentitu goiza aurpegian,
Goibel gaudenean dena irizten zaigu ospel,
Adoretsu gaudenean, atzera, papurtu egiten da mundua.
Denok gordetzen dugu betiko besteren alde ezkutu bat,
Dela sekretua, dela akatsa, dela keinua.
Erdu eta larrutuko ditugu irabazleak,
Zubitik jauzi egin geure buruaz barre.
Isilik begiratuko diegu portuko garabiei,
Elkarrekin isilik egotea baita
adiskidetasunaren frogarik behinena.
Erdu nirekin, herriz aldatu nahi dut,
Nire gorputz hau albo batera utzi
Eta maskor batean zurekin sartu,
Gure txikitasunarekin, mangolinoak bezala.
Erdu, zure zain nago,
Duela urtebete etendako istorioa jarraituko dugu,
Ibai ondoko urki zuriek uztai bat gehiago ez balute bezala.

Dylan Thomas said,
but she does sometimes,
and my father's life flickered away like that,

headed westwards
into the horizon like a ship and vanished
leaving a wake of memories.


**MAY**
> *Let me look into your eyes.*
> *I want to know how you are.*
> Rainer W. Fassbinder


Look, May is here,
its blue eyelid all over the port.
Come, I haven't heard from you for so long,
you seem frightened, like the kittens we drowned.
Come, let's talk about the usual stuff,
about how it's better to be kind,
about having to live with doubt,
about filling the voids within.
Come, feel the morning on your face,
everything is so bleak when we're low,
and yet the world is insignificant come high times.
We always hide part of ourselves from others.
A secret, a fault, a gesture.
Come, let's tear the winners to shreds,
let's laugh ourselves off the bridge,
let's watch the port pulleys in silence,
because being silent together
is the utmost proof of friendship.
Come with me, I want to live elsewhere,
leave this body behind
and inhabit another shell with you,
enjoy our smallness, like winkles do.
Come, I am waiting,
let's continue the story we interrupted a year ago,
as if those silver birches don't have a ring more.

PHOTO: TARN McDONALD

AMAIA GABANTXO is a literary translator, writer and reviewer. Her work has appeared in journals such as *Modern Poetry in Translation, Pretext, The Atlanta Review, Metamorphoses* and *Transcript,* as well as in the *Times Literary Supplement* and *The Independent* and in anthologies such as *An Anthology of Basque Short Stories* (University of Nevada Press, 2004) and *Spain: A Traveler's Literary Companion* (Berkeley, California: Whereabouts Press, 2004). She is the translator of Anjel Lertxundi's *Perfect Happiness* (University of Nevada Press, 2007) and, at the time of writing, is translating Unai Elorriaga's *Vredaman* (New York: Archipelago Books, 2007) and Laura Mintegi's *Ecce Homo* (Txalaparta, 2008). She has written for multi-cultural, multimedia art projects both in England and the Basque Country, and taken part in poetry festivals in London and Dublin.

She lives in Norwich, where she is completing a PhD in the School of Literature and Creative Writing at the University of East Anglia. She has been awarded a Wingate Scholarship, received the Jury's Commendation in the BCLA Literary Translation Competition and been short-listed for the Asham Short Story Prize.

She moonlights as a flamenco singer.

PHOTO: AUTHOR'S ARCHIVE

MARI JOSE OLAZIREGI was born in Donostia in 1963 and holds a PhD in Basque literature. She is a lecturer at the University of the Basque Country (Vitoria-Gasteiz, Spain). She also has an MA on the Promotion of Reading Habits from the Ramon Llull University (Barcelona), and is currently completing an MA in Studies in Fiction at the University of East Anglia (UK). In 1997, Dr. Olaziregi was awarded the Becerro de Bengoa Prize for the essay 'Bernardo Atxagaren irakurlea' (Bernardo Atxaga's Reader). Since 2003, she has been the editor of the Basque Literature in Translation Series at the Center for Basque Studies (University of Nevada, Reno) and the director of the www.basqueliterature.com website. She has written numerous forewords for Basque novels and anthologies, and published essays in international journals, some of which have been translated into English, French, Spanish, Czech, Slovenian and Italian. She specialises in contemporary Basque literature and is renowned for her critical work on Bernardo Atxaga. She is the author of seven books on Basque literature; among them *Euskal eleberriaren historia* (History of the Basque Novel, 2001), and *Waking the Hedgehog: The Literary Universe of Bernardo Atxaga*, (University of Nevada Press, 2005, translated from Basque by Amaia Gabantxo). She has edited anthologies such as: *Etzikoak: Antologija sodobne baskovske knjizesnosti*, published in Slovenian in 2006 and *An Anthology of Basque Short Stories* (2004) which has been translated into Spanish, Russian and Italian.

Marijo Olaziregi was a member of IBBY's executive committee in 2004-2006 and has been a member of the Royal Academy of the Basque Language since 2000. She is the editor of *A History of Basque Literature*.

PHOTO: AUTHOR'S ARCHIVE

ALEXANDRA BÜCHLER was born in Prague and was educated there, in Thessaloniki, Greece, and Melbourne, Australia. She has lived in Great Britain since 1989. She is founding director of Literature Across Frontiers, a programme of international literary exchange based in the UK, and a member of the editorial board of its European Internet Review of Books and Writing, *Transcript*. A translator of fiction, poetry, theatre plays and texts on modern art and architecture from English, Czech and Greek, she has published over twenty-five works, including books by such authors as J. M. Coetzee, David Malouf, Jean Rhys, Janice Galloway and Rhea Galanaki in Czech translation. She has also edited and part-translated a number of anthologies, including *This Side of Reality: Modern Czech Writing* (1996), *Allskin and Other Tales by Contemporary Czech Women* (1998) and the most recent *A Fine Line: New Poetry from Eastern and Central Europe* (Arc Publications, 2004).

Other anthologies of poetry in translation
published by Arc Publications
include:

*Altered State: An Anthology of New Polish Poetry*
EDS. ROD MENGHAM, TADEUSZ PIÓRO, PIOTR SZYMOR
Translated by Rod Mengham, Tadeusz Pióro *et al*

*A Fine Line: New Poetry from Eastern*
*& Central Europe*
EDS. JEAN BOASE-BEIER, ALEXANDRA BÜCHLER, FIONA SAMPSON
Various translators

*6 Slovenian Poets*
ED. BRANE MOZETIČ
Translated by Ana Jelnikar, Kelly Lennox Allen
& Stephen Watts, with an introduction by
Aleš Debeljak
NO. 1 IN THE 'NEW VOICES FROM EUROPE & BEYOND' ANTHOLOGY SERIES,
SERIES EDITOR: ALEXANDRA BÜCHLER